P9-DVD-592

DATE DUE

C. M
9/93

DE 9 9?			

Demco, Inc. 38-293

Wild Ice

Riverside Community College
Library
4800 Magnolia Avenue
Riverside, California 92506

© 1990 by the Smithsonian Institution
All rights reserved

LIBRARY OF CONGRESS CATALOGING-IN-PUBLICATION DATA

Wild ice : Antarctic journeys / Ron Naveen . . . [et al.].
p.   cm.
ISBN 0–87474–395–8 (alk. paper).
1. Antarctic regions.   I. Naveen, Ron.
G860.W55   1990
919.8'9—dc20   89–26268

British Library Cataloguing-in-Publication Data is available
Printed in Italy
97 96 95 94 93 92 91 90   5 4 3 2 1

The paper used in this publication meets the minimum
requirements of the American National Standard
for Permanence of Paper for Printed Library Materials Z39.48–1984

For permission to reproduce photographs appearing in this
book, please correspond directly with the authors, whose
initials listed in the individual captions indicate ownership.
The Smithsonian Institution Press does not retain
reproduction rights for these photographs individually.

RON NAVEEN | COLIN MONTEATH | TUI DE ROY | MARK JONES

WILD ICE

Antarctic Journeys

Smithsonian Institution Press   Washington and London

To Ellen and Alex   RON NAVEEN

To Marion, Betty, Denali, and Carys Monteath
for love and endless support during journeys South
COLIN MONTEATH

To my dear Mom and Dad, for your
understanding of the different path my life has taken,
and for your constant love despite the distances which
separate our worlds; thank you for giving me the abilities
and desires to seek the best in this world
MARK JONES

To all my friends, finned, furry, and feathered,
and to those dear humans who brought me into this world,
and helped me learn how to respect them all
TUI DE ROY

Together we dedicate this book to the fervent hope that
Antarctica and its surrounding Southern Ocean ecosystem
shall remain wild and free forever

*Opening photo sequence: p. 1, an adult
king penguin (MJ); pp. 2–3, breeding
ground of Adélie penguins on Torgersen
Island (CM); pp. 4–5, light reflections on
the Lemaire Channel (RN); pp. 6–7,
immense tabular bergs calved from
Antarctica's ice shelves (CM); pp. 8–9, the
Vinson Massif, the highest point in
Antarctica at 4,897 meters (CM); pp. 10–
11, Adélie penguins at Cape Royds, the
most southerly penguin rookery in
Antarctica (CM).*

Contents

HRH Prince Edward at Ross Island. (CM)

Foreword

It is virtually impossible to describe Antarctica accurately to anybody who hasn't been there. I know—scientists and researchers tried to describe it to me before I saw it for the first time in 1982. They told me it was a land of extremes; the coldest, driest, windiest, highest continent in the world. They showed me as many photographs as they could and told me as many anecdotes as they wanted me to hear, but it still didn't adequately prepare me for the experience of being on "the ice."

Now that I have been there I can fully appreciate what they mean and why "the ice" holds such a fascination for them. By "them" I mean all those who have had the good fortune to have experienced raw nature at its breathtakingly beautiful best.

There are other places in the world where nature stuns, amazes, or utterly dominates man's achievements, but there are few places where all these forces combine. Antarctica is a continent that continually humbles man and not least man's greed.

Antarctica was seen as, and recognized as, a scientific park, embodied in the Antarctic Treaty of 1959. For thirty years the principal signatories have maintained and adhered to the spirit of that treaty, recognizing both the value and the fragility of the continent. That fragility could be broken if totally unnecessary and potentially damaging commercial exploitation is allowed.

This book should give you an insight into the life of this great continent. Most important, I hope it helps you understand it.

His Royal Highness
Prince Edward

Preface

One hundred fifty million years ago, the supercontinent Gondwana dominated the earth's surface. As tectonic movement shifted the great plates composing this vast land mass, the continents began to move and, about 37 million years ago, the Drake Passage between South America and Antarctica began to form. The great Antarctic ecosystem breathed its first life.

Antarctica's proportions are enormous: it contains 5.4 million square miles, equivalent to 10 percent of the earth's land surface and approximately the size of the United States and Mexico combined. During the austral winter, sea ice at least doubles the size of the continent. Ninety-nine percent of Antarctica is covered by a permanent ice sheet, which averages over a mile in thickness, and in some places is almost three miles thick. Ninety percent of the world's ice and 70 percent of the world's fresh water is locked in this ice pack. Antarctica's surrounding Southern Ocean ecosystem is the largest and most fertile in the world. It comprises 13.9 million square miles, equivalent to 10 percent of the world's oceans, and extends from the Antarctic continent to the Antarctic Convergence, that boundary where northward-moving, cold Antarctic water meets southward-flowing, warm subantarctic water from the Atlantic, Pacific, and Indian oceans. The Antarctic circumpolar current—the West Wind Drift—transports more water than any other system in the world's oceans. The sheer richness of the ecosystem is staggering.

As this book is published, that ecosystem begins its fourth decade of oversight by the Antarctic Treaty system. The Antarctic Treaty was signed in 1959 (and went into force two years later) amid a rampant feeling of worldwide goodwill generated by the International Geophysical Year. Today more than 75 percent of the earth's population is represented in the Antarctic Treaty system, which continues to protect a continent devoted to science and our own species' best instincts. In great part, the entire system is built on an internal compromise that allowed seven claimant nations (as well as the United States and the Soviet Union,

(Opposite)

Late summer twilight bathes the snow-clad mountains of the Danco Coast. Under the shadowy cliffs of tiny Couverville Island, kelp gulls stand watch. The Gerlache Strait provides a bonanza of food for whales, seals, and seabirds during the short summer. (TDR)

A chinstrap penguin awaits evening at Half Moon Island, Antarctic Peninsula. Why the chinstrap? We don't know, although the strap is prominently featured when the penguin displays ecstatically to its mate, with beak raised high to the sky, head waving from side to side, wings gesticulating strongly up and down, and the bird braying loudly and hoarsely. (RN)

which assert the "basis" for such claims) to avoid pressing their territorial instincts to the maximum. Now that there has already been one war in the Southern Ocean, the preciousness of that internal compromise has become ever more apparent.

The treaty has maintained its status as a modern-day Magna Carta by closing real or apparent gaps in its original version. Whales are now protected under the adjunct International Whaling Convention, and the Antarctic Treaty parties have implemented separate conventions regarding the conservation of Antarctic seals and of marine living resources (krill and fish). As this fourth decade begins, the treaty parties are debating another gap: oil, gas, and minerals. Whether by a new convention to strictly regulate any future development, by changes to the present Agreed Measures protecting flora and fauna under the existing treaty, or by a new comprehensive environmental regime, the parties must sort through this latest controversy with vigor and purpose. Again, the goal should be accomplishing the necessary environmental protection while preserving that delicate internal compromise that has kept the Antarctic a demilitarized, denuclearized continent for peace, wildlife, and science.

Oceanites, Inc., a nonprofit educational foundation devoted to raising the public's awareness of the oceans and their resources, is pleased to be associated with *Wild Ice*. Not only as a coauthor/photographer, but also as the editor of Oceanites's newsletter, *The Antarctic Century*, I take particular satisfaction in the publication of this inspirational volume. My personal and charitable purposes have merged, and I relish the expectation that *Wild Ice* will foster more "Antarctic spirit." Both this book and the lives of the four of us who participated in its creation have been molded by Antarctica's rich history and legacy. The serenity and pristine qualities of the great seventh continent and its surrounding ocean ecosystem must continue. Antarctica is where our dreams and aspirations lie. It is where we must continue evidencing that particular brand of goodwill and caring so typical of us *Homo sapiens*.

Looking into the crystal ball, however, one sees grim portents. The world's population has already passed 5.5 billion and will reach 12 billion before the middle of the next century. We humans may have exceeded—artificially—our own carrying capacity on this planet and, if the trend is not reversed, even Antarctica will be consumed by our never-ending, sometimes wrong-headed search for food and fuel. Global warming may have started, posing potentially calamitous consequences for the Wild Ice. More immediately, the diminishment of the protective ozone layer above the Antarctic has been linked, disturbingly, to reduced phytoplankton and zooplankton production. This may mean less food for krill—the Antarctic's "power lunch"—and, ultimately, less food for krill's major consumers.

Humankind, let alone treaty systems, cannot easily regulate morality or environmental purity. But perhaps we can be inspired to higher ground. If not, we as a species are doomed, as are our fellow travelers on this planet—the penguins, whales, krill, and seals—and our beloved Antarctica itself. I'm struck by the "gray matter" that these monumental issues present. They pose no clear, black-and-white solutions, nor will any of our difficult choices be cheap. But they must be made.

We must band together to inspire ourselves, our policymakers, and our friends. Clearly, the risk of becoming an "Antarcticist"—to use Apsley Cherry-Garrard's term—is that it generates serious responsibilities and obligations. Fortunately, being an optimist, I believe that our serious band of Antarcticists can change the world and ensure that the Wild Ice remains wild, forever.

Ron Naveen
President, Oceanites, Inc.
Cooksville, Maryland

Acknowledgments

In 1922 Apsley Cherry-Garrard wrote in *The Worst Journey in the World*, his time-honored account of experiences during Scott's 1910–14 expedition, that "polar exploration is at once the cleanest and most isolated way of having a bad time which has ever been devised."

Half a century later, this has not proven to be the case for this book's coauthors. In making over sixty journeys to Antarctica we have become totally enthralled by the majesty and wildness of the continent. We have all been extremely fortunate to have had deeply moving experiences over the years while in pursuit of science, high-spirited adventure, or nature photography. These journeys have changed our lives.

All four of us have met and traveled with dozens of remarkable characters from far-flung corners of the globe, each of whom in his or her own way was inescapably drawn to Antarctica. Many of these people have assisted us during past expeditions or during the production of this book.

We wish to express our sincere appreciation to the field scientists and administrators of the U.S., British, and New Zealand Antarctic Programs. On the U.S. side, we are much appreciative of the cooperation and friendship of colleagues in the Department of State, the National Marine Fisheries Service, and the National Science Foundation. Many thanks to Peter Prince and John Croxall of the British Antarctic Survey for their cooperation and special efforts in maintaining a flow of up-to-date scientific papers and information. A note of special gratitude to Captain T. L. M. Sunter and to all of the men—past, present, and future—of the British ice patrol ship HMS *Endurance* for their comradeship, loyalty, passion, and Antarctic spirit.

Each of us has journeyed to Antarctica with tour companies that have pioneered and furthered an important concept: the simple appreciation of earth's wildest continent. To Society Expeditions, Salen Lindblad Cruising, Lindblad Travel, and Adventure Network International we extend thanks for their continued support and the high standard of their

(Opposite)

Sunset light bathes Mount Scott in the Lemaire Channel. (CM)

There is little wonder why penguins—in this case, some Adélies—generate such enthusiasm among their observers. Their often comical struts and waddles on land combine pomposity with exuberance. (MJ)

leadership in educational Antarctic tourism. We are deeply grateful to our colleagues during these ventures, a multitude of ZAPS, SODS, and SOWS without whose assistance many of *Wild Ice*'s images would not have been possible.

Our particular thanks go to Allan Borut, Barbara Heffernan, Martha Muse, Renate Rennie, Tom McIntyre, Susan Drennan, Frank Todd, Peter Harrison, Susan and Wayne Trivelpiece, Mike McDowell, Susan and Werner Zehnder, William Evans, Jim Caffin, Peter Cleary, Bob Mc-Kerrow, Paul Broady, Peter Barrett, and Kathy Cashman for the personal impetus they have provided to our many Antarctic ventures.

There are many other friends from around the world—too numerous to list—whose help we can never forget, friends who have taken the time to critique and direct our development in photography and writing.

We are grateful to our acquisitions editor at Smithsonian Institution Press, Peter Cannell, for his enthusiasm about our project, and to the entire Press staff for their support, interest, and excitement about *Wild Ice*.

Ultimately, *Wild Ice* would not have been possible without the advice and generous assistance of two very special friends—individuals who have themselves tasted the raw beauty of Antarctica. They too have become inspired and committed to protect its integrity and wildness. We sincerely hope this book will help further their dream. Thank you.

Large icebergs often strand over shallow rocks, impeding their path to the open sea. (TDR)

RON NAVEEN

At the Edge, and Beyond

Like a magnet I was pulled, caught in a lustful pursuit that dispelled my usual deliberate caution. From high above, the albatross's solicitation was prolonged and clearly seductive: mournful, trumpeting cries of "p'yarrr–eee, p'yarrr–eee" that boomed loudly over Royal Bay's extended reaches, drawing me upward and eerily suggesting the ghosts of this island's lustrous past. I had returned to my spiritual home and, true to form, was immediately into the thick of it.

Visually and emotionally, the island of South Georgia overwhelms. At first glance, it resembles the far South Atlantic branch of Dr. Doolittle's fantastic zoo: a profusion of captivating animals that quickly transforms even the most discriminating observer into a raving anthropomorphic. Its conglomeration of dark peaks; white glaciers, snow, and ice; green tussock, grasses, and mosses; brown mud and bogs; and colorful animals suggests no landscape that the masters' brushes have rendered. Its mountains have been dubbed the "Alps of the Southern Ocean," and its surrounding waters, save for the now decimated whales, remain among the world's richest. One final ingredient—a swashbuckling history of high seas adventures, trials, and tribulations—adds to the romance.

If Antarctica and the Southern Ocean are the crown—the last relatively pristine ecosystem on earth—then the subantarctic outcrops rimming the seventh continent are this tiara's shining jewels: South Georgia, Bouvet, Macquarie, Enderby, Snares, Auckland. All are rich introductions to the vast repository of wildlife, history, dreams, and emotions metaphorically dubbed the Deep South, The Ice, or, more graphically, the Wild Ice. These islands lie along the Antarctic's mobile, northern boundary, which is called the Convergence. This is where subfreezing Antarctic water meets warmer subantarctic water from the Atlantic, Pacific, and Indian oceans (generally located between 47 and 63 degrees south latitude), in an upwelling zone of rich nutrients thrust upward from the depths. Below the line, *Euphausia superba*, the shrimplike crustacean that fuels the entire Antarctic ecosystem, dominates the food chain. Every-

(Opposite)

Even king penguins seem to enjoy their extraordinary surroundings. The great Weddell Glacier at the foot of Royal Bay on the island of South Georgia imparts a spectacular luster to an overwhelming array of snow-capped peaks, dense mosses and grasses, and dizzying numbers of king penguins and seals. (RN)

(Overleaf)

In the pounding surf on the northwestern end of St. Andrew's Bay, South Georgia, two king penguins nuzzle each other in their engaging neck-wrapping style. (RN)

The Antarctic is the south Atlantic branch of Dr. Doolittle's fantastic zoo, offering an engaging array of animals and animal assemblages. Here, a group of king penguins relaxes and basks on the beach at St. Andrew's Bay, South Georgia. (RN)

one—whales, penguins, and even human fishermen—exploits these tiny animals, which are spectacularly nutritious, containing up to 20 percent protein when wet (and up to 80 percent protein when dried). No doubt about it, krill are the Deep South's power lunch.

This enormous Antarctic and Southern Ocean ecosystem is the largest and most fertile on earth: 14 million square miles, equal to 10 percent of the world's oceans, and extending from the Antarctic continent to the Antarctic Convergence. The richness is staggering: an annual production of phytoplankton and microplankton that may reach 6,400 million tons; 33 million seals weighing 7 million tons; 500 thousand whales weighing 9 million tons; at least 75 million penguins and seabirds weighing at least 400 million tons; and anywhere from 100 to 700 million tons of krill. One estimate suggests 500 million tons of krill being taken annually by seabirds, whales, seals, fish, squid, and other predators.

Yet these animals and life forms are mere pieces in a vast, complex jigsaw puzzle that somehow fits together—unforgettably, harmoniously. The resulting mosaic fills the recesses of one's memory; the island's gestalt is a panoply of spectacular dreams come true.

Throughout the year, South Georgia sits below the Convergence, a lonely outcrop in the middle of a protein extravaganza. Dimensionally, it runs about 105 miles from northwest to southeast, ranging from just over 1 mile to 19 miles in width. It is 340 miles from the Sandwich Islands to the east, 1,250 miles from the South American coast to the west, 640 miles from the South Orkney Islands to the south, and 960 miles from the nearest point on the Antarctic continent. Its surface area encompasses almost 1,500 square miles, more than half of which is covered by permanent ice and snow.

The resident human population is zero, the penguin, seabird, and seal population is rather boundless, and the resulting minority status for *Homo sapiens* does wonders for one's psyche. This far-flung outpost lacks contrails in the sky, rock music in the streets, garbage in the landscape, and blathering politicians immersed in inconsequential minutiae. In their stead, one's ears tune quickly to the whistling and calling king penguins, the bleating, growling fur seals, and the belching, grunting, and defecating southern elephant seals. (The belching is extraordinary, suggesting that these "ellies" suffer from the worst imaginable cases of indigestion or gastroenteritis.) South Georgia is for contemplative types, offering refuge from the schisms of daily existence on our crowded planet, circa 2000. Some say that if God ever wanted a vacation, he (or she) would go to South Georgia.

I came not for vacation, but to count penguins, find seabird burrows, and further catalog South Georgia's abundant fauna. This particular, early December day in Royal Bay was unusually clear, and I had high hopes for some up-close-and-personal encounters with a favorite obsession, the sleek and mysterious light-mantled sooty albatross. It was my seventh visit to South Georgia, but the first during the early austral summer when light-mantled sooties are in full courtship display. On the beach near the helicopter landing site, I bid adieu to hundreds of king penguins and scores of elephant seals, crossed westward through a nar-

The northern coast of rugged South Georgia Island is a major breeding ground for king penguins. Although aspects of the South Georgia environment are subantarctic in nature, the island lies south of the Antarctic Convergence and hence is truly part of Antarctica. (CM)

27

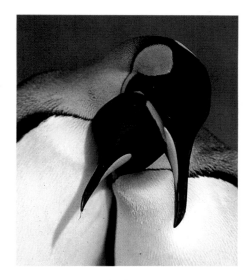

Above: Kings and other penguins spend considerable time reinforcing their pair bonds, partly out of faithfulness to their nest sites. (TDR) *Opposite: King penguin rookeries defy description—bodies everywhere, snow-capped peaks above, green and brown tones in between.* (RN)

King penguin chicks take up to 300 days or more to fledge, requiring considerable attention from parents and preventing them from successfully raising a chick more often than two out of every three years. (TDR)

row pass toward the bay's primary king colony and beyond a magnificent cascading waterfall, then veered upslope at the first opportunity.

Moment to more difficult moment, I trudged skyward, scrambling over talus outcrops, using the slippery but strongly rooted tussock plants for handholds. Finally towering almost 200 feet above the plain, I realized that, foolishly, I had ignored the severity of the suddenly crumpling slope and the precariously narrow ledge that I had reached. The winged prophet was so close, yet still so enticingly beyond my tussock-restricted sight. I'd gone too far and suddenly I couldn't move. Above, what looked like a clear path had vanished; down, my toeholds were obscured by the treacherous angle. As I faced in to the slope, noisy, swirling gusts of wind accentuated my chest's pounding; my sweat began to run like glacial melt.

With free fall pending, thoughts soared wildly, becoming dazzling specks that danced across my mind's eye: Ernest Shackleton in his death throes at Grytviken; whalers and sealers whose dreams of fame and fortune sank in these freezing waters; a picture-postcard, fairytale landscape almost beyond the power of language to describe. Here I was, a veritable flea speck amidst countless numbers of penguins, albatrosses, seals, and other organisms, lost among the huge green tussock clumps, surrounded by the geological glitter of snow-capped peaks, glaciers, icebergs, and still-to-be discovered evidence of this planet's evolution.

Maybe Antarctica *was* God, my imminent demise simply confirming the unyielding, pantheistic scheme. Approaching delusion, I smiled at the thousands of incubating king penguins massed tightly below, fallaciously confident that their soft security blanket of white, gray, and orange would gently break my plunge. On the ledge, prudence fortunately maintained a grip: I determined to hold on, relax, and try to find a way out.

King penguin rookeries are beautiful settings that change constantly: fog rolling in and back, sun appearing and disappearing, penguins strutting continually to the sea and back. (RN)

Sir Ernest had always found a way out. He was a brilliant leader who never lost a man under his direct command. "The Boss" was loved by his men and deified by his peers; Amundsen, Byrd, and Gould pored over Shackleton's diaries to inspire and guide their own grand adventures in The Ice. If there was regret, it was that Shackleton never seemed to achieve the goals his expeditions sought; he was plagued by huge predicaments that always turned his expeditions into feats of survival.

In 1907 Shackleton turned back from the South Pole, only eighty-seven miles away, to ensure his team's safe return. Amundsen and Scott then claimed the Pole for their own respective destinies. In 1915, even before getting the chance to start his trans-Antarctic crossing, Shackleton's ship *Endurance* was hopelessly beset in the Weddell Sea pack; when the ship was crushed, he moved his men onto the ice, then into the lifeboats, ultimately reaching the far-flung yet relatively safe Elephant Island. A land camp was established. There were many penguins and seals to eat, but the team was 800 miles from the nearest humanity, South Georgia's north shore whaling stations. From Elephant, Shackleton and five colleagues embarked on the greatest open-boat voyage of all time, miraculously navigating the stormy ocean to South Georgia's southern coast. Then came an impassioned and dangerous thirty-six-hour climb over the island's peaks, after which Shackleton, Crean, and Worsley walked down the broad valley into the Stromness whaling station and, for the first time in two years, into the grasp of civilization. After a few misses, Shackleton returned to rescue his twenty-two comrades who, under the command of Frank Wild, had never given up hope that "today's the day the Boss might come."

South Georgia is laced with such memories of Shackleton. At the sheltered harbor of Grytviken in Cumberland Bay on the central north coast, a white hillside cross commemorates the Boss's memory and greets each visitor. And it is here, near the site of one of the island's largest whaling stations, that Sir Ernest is buried. A short, albeit muddy, walk leads from the detritus of the station's rusting metal and machinery to Grytviken's lovely cemetery, tucked on a hillside with a grand view to the north toward the open bay and the seas beyond. Elephant seals assemble en masse within inches of the cemetery's collapsing fence, snorting, bellowing, and occasionally rearing their massive hulks. A few king penguins always seem to be about, molting or resting in the wet and oozing bogs. Above the plots and south toward the interior looms Mount Paget, the island's tallest peak, often obscured by the endlessly changing weather and clouds.

The Boss

(Opposite)

King penguins make no nests; instead they incubate their eggs on the tops of their feet. As a result, once the young are old enough to be free from their parents' protection, colonies are always in perpetual motion, with individuals shuffling about here and there. Because the breeding cycle is over a year long, within a single colony there can be individuals at all stages of reproduction: courting pairs, incubating adults, young chicks, or molting juveniles. Certain groupings do occur, however, as is the case with these yearling chicks. (MJ)

(Opposite)

Antarctica is not the stark black-and-white continent imprinted on the minds of many. The combination of a low sun angle and a clear atmosphere often produces dazzling colors. (RN)

The cemetery is a sacred resting ground for whalers, sealers, and one young Argentinian who died during the recent Southern Ocean War. The Shackleton tombstone dominates, a narrow, tall granite monument on the innermost edge toward the hillside. Plaquettes from scores of vessels, representing many nationalities, line its base. The monument's reverse side is inscribed with a paraphrase from one of Sir Ernest's favorite poems, Browning's "The Statue and the Bust," a calling card for those who seek adventure and are lured by The Ice: "A man should strive to the uttermost for his life's set prize."

For Shackleton, that prize was the glory and ardor of Antarctic exploration. Try after try, failure after failure, Shackleton persevered. Years after the failures of his South Pole attempt and his trans-Antarctic crossing, Shackleton returned one last time in 1918 on the *Quest.* On anchor at Grytviken, with the mission hardly under way, Shackleton lay in bed one evening, totally enthralled by one particularly bright star shining above. As his pain increased, he summoned Macklin, the ship's doctor; Shackleton had successfully hidden his heart-related infirmities from almost everyone, including his men, but now his time had come. Just forty-eight years old, he practically died in Macklin's arms, still balking and complaining about the good doc's admonitions to take better care of self and body.

Hemingway claimed that the most common degree of bravery is the temporary ability to ignore possible consequences. Then, with exhilaration, comes a more pronounced degree: not to give a damn for possible consequences and not just to ignore them, but rather to despise them. This aptly describes the Boss; he challenged geography and science for secrets yet uncovered, battled ceaselessly for his men, but basically cared not one whit for his own self.

I've often taken expedition participants to the Grytviken cemetery, to recount the Boss's great deeds and this inspiring history. T. S. Eliot's poem *The Waste Land,* inspired by Shackleton, sets the tone:

> *Who is the third who walks always beside you?*
> *When I count, there are only you and I together*
> *But when I look ahead up the white road*
> *There is always another one walking beside you*
> *Gliding wrapt in a brown mantle, hooded*
> *I do not know whether a man or a woman*
> *—But who is that on the other side of you?*

While crossing the South Georgian mountains, Shackleton envisioned that he was being watched, perhaps protected, by some unknown spirit.

The moon rises over a berg in the Gerlache Strait of the Antarctic Peninsula. In the quietude of the Antarctic, one feels that one is in the midst of life's processes, not a passive participant in the changing world. The scenes are striking, as if one was viewing earth at a primitive time, perhaps as Antarctica may have looked after separating from Gondwana 37 million years ago. (RN)

He wasn't a religious man, but he couldn't shake the sensation of invisible comradeship; he had no explanation for his damned good luck in surviving both the treacherous open boat voyage from Elephant Island and the incredible thirty-six-hour hike from King Haakon Bay to Stromness (only replicated recently by a British Joint Services team). As described in his book *South:*

When I look back at those days I have no doubt that Providence guided us, not only across those snowfields, but across the snow-white sea that separated Elephant Island from our landing-place on South Georgia. I know that during that long and racking march of thirty-six hours over the unnamed mountains and glaciers of South Georgia it seemed to me often that we were four, not three. I said nothing to my companions on the point, but afterwards Worsley said to me, "Boss, I had a curious feeling on the march that there was another person with us." Crean confessed to the same idea. One feels "the dearth of human words, the roughness of mortal speech" in trying to describe things intangible, but a record of our journeys would be incomplete without a reference to a subject very near to our hearts.

While Shackleton found some of these intangibles difficult to describe, other experiences aroused his own poetry and allowed him to crystallize the special grandeur that he'd been privileged to touch:

In memories we were rich. We had pierced the veneer of outside things. We had suffered, starved, and triumphed, grovelled, yet grasped at glory, grown bigger in the bigness of the whole. We had seen God in his splendours, heard the text that Nature renders. We had reached the naked soul of man.

Heroes

For more than three centuries, South Georgia's naked soul has been the target of numerous intrepid characters. It was the jumping-off spot for many Antarctic explorers and scientists and the base for Southern Ocean sealing and land-based whaling operations. More recently, it was a battleground in the Southern Ocean War, the British and Argentinians fighting major skirmishes on its soil and waters. It has been suggested that the bells in Grytviken's little white chapel used to mourn whales and seals; now they've also tolled for the folly of intractable humans.

South Georgia's impressive list of visitors includes Antoine de la Roche, perhaps its first discoverer, in 1675; Captain James Cook, who made his first landing on the island in 1775, and who returned twice more; the first sealers, in 1786; Russian admiral Fabian Gottlieb von Bellingshausen, in 1819; James Weddell, in 1823; the brig *Daisy,* commanded by Captain Benjamin Cleveland, and carrying the great ornithologist Robert Cushman Murphy, in 1912–13; and, in 1904, Captain C. A. Larsen, whose arrival marked the beginning of the island's whaling operations.

These adventurers came south for fame and fortune; some found it and others died for the trying, but none claimed passivity about the experience. South Georgia changed lives. The history inevitably focuses on South Georgia's once flourishing but now defunct (since 1964–65) whaling operations. The central north coast is dotted with many pro-

tected harbors, bays, and anchorages, where the remnants of these once-burgeoning whale factories—Leith, Stromness, Grytviken, Husvik, Prince Olav Harbor—lie in rust. In a span of more than sixty years, these stations processed between one-half to two-thirds of the Southern Ocean's whales, turning these creatures into oil and other now decidedly unnecessary products; in little more than a century, the fur seals were brought to extinction's brink. Some say that the ghosts of whalers and sealers haunt the island, and an eerie presence accompanies one's stroll past the dormant flensing platforms and killing beaches that once bustled with activity.

At Stromness, the chalkboard of daily counts still stands, the names "Sei, Sperm, Fin" and others remaining legible on the upward horizontal row. Inside the huge hangar, the machinery is stilled, the storage rooms hold hundreds of unused metal sheets and plates, and broken glass litters the floor. The smell is gone, but the air is thick with the past.

Beyond this huge building stands the white house of the Stromness station manager, where Shackleton and his weary hikers found help and bathed for the first time in years. Outside, a small group of reindeer browses lichens on the station's periphery, near ramshackle, crumbling structures that the sluglike elephant seals have reoccupied. Entering the darkened buildings requires some fortitude, because the ellies like to greet appearances with unnerving barrages of whoops and belches.

I've often climbed the green and burnt sienna hills behind Stromness to get a full view of this striking fjord, but also to confront the invisible comradeship that I share with the old whalers and sealers. I admit great difficulty in trying to judge them; while today we can recognize the ultimate folly of their mass rendering, we must also accept that they worked in a different era with much different prevailing attitudes and circumstances. They faced more of South Georgia's dire weather and frightful seas than I would ever care to encounter. But facts are facts: gross numbers of animals died in these industries, and it is unclear whether or not the whales will ever recover. In the seas beyond, there used to be the blows and fluke slaps of thousands; now innumerable blanched bones are scattered in open repose around the beaches.

On the upside, however, South Georgia pulsates these days with the shuffles and undulations of southern elephant seal and Kerguelen fur seal multitudes; the latter vastly exceed their former numbers. The fur seals' fusiform shapes are common offshore sights everywhere, particularly on South Georgia's northwestern end where the density is extraordinary. I can attest to their comeback, having almost been chewed too many times by musky "wigs" (the large, harem-collecting male fur

(Opposite)

Elephant seals joust for supremacy. This ritual fighting is a fact of life among males who, ultimately, must win select areas of turf on the beaches to attract willing females in their harem-oriented society. (TDR)

(Overleaf)

A small proportion of the Kerguelen fur seal population exhibits a light color phase. These morphs are not albinos, and it is not believed that their blonder appearance disadvantages them in any way from their future participation in the species' harem society. (CM)

A pilgrim elephant seal reclaims turf at the now-abandoned Stromness whaling station, South Georgia. Human consumers now turn toward a much smaller product, krill, the small crustacean that is the power lunch of the Antarctic ecosystem. (RN)

Kerguelen fur seals have made a remarkable comeback in the subantarctic fringe north of the Antarctic Peninsula. Being on the receiving end of their fearsome growls suggests that we should condemn future overexploitations to the depths of nonrepetitive history. (RN)

Young elephant seals fight on the beach at Gold Harbor, South Georgia. These sparring matches provide early training for future bouts to control the most numbers of females and the most prized waterfront territories. (RN)

An elephant seal basks in a kelp bed. Despite their enormous, half-ton size and growling utterances, these animals produce endearing poses. (TDR)

43

seals). But being on the receiving end is instructive. As consumptive human eyes turn to the protein-rich krill in these waters, perhaps the legacy of the whalers and sealers will be an enlightenment, one that condemns overexploitation to the depths of nonrepetitive history.

Natty Hairdos and the Lives of Kings

The seals offer literal and metaphorical evidence that South Georgia is crawling with animals. Their profusion is matched by South Georgia's bounteous and highly engaging penguins, which arouse one's senses to new extremes: eyes can hardly believe the Chaplinesque histrionics of these avian waddlers and swimmers; noses inflate with the nitrogenous perfume of these animals' excrement and crowded living conditions; eardrums ache painfully from the splitting, pounding noises of their rookeries. As with a long-remembered feast, penguins sentimentally tug at the soul and produce smiles long after the act of consumption.

The island's most numerous penguin by far—perhaps up to 6 million breeding pairs—is the macaroni, belonging to the family *Eudyptes,* which generally possess long yellow-orange locks and tufts on their heads. This particular species is named for the old hairdo memorialized in the song "Yankee Doodle Dandy" ("stuck a feather in his cap and called it macaroni"). Their blood-red eyes and massive, light-pinkish bills add a demonic aspect to their appearance.

For the researcher, macs pose a considerable challenge. Their preferred habitat is steep, rocky, uphill slopes, which are generally impossible to reach by human foot; to exit to the sea, macs usually face a smashing surf and the threat of submerged rocks. Obviously, they're not faint-hearted. On my own terms, I have mixed feelings about "working" mac colonies: on these inaccessible slopes it's difficult to maintain one's balance; worse, one is inevitably in close proximity to some of the strongest, most dangerous beaks in the business. Macs are master ankle chompers, and one often suffers a multitude of scrapes, bruises, and bites. Beneath this bird's beautiful, flowing tufts lies the disposition of a bulldog, a pit bull of the tussock, your basic attack penguin! In mac land, the grating cacaphony drowns the howling wind and smashing surf, and imprints a long-lasting sound track of honking static.

Macs, like their *Eudyptid* cousins (the so-called "crested" penguins), have a curious breeding strategy. Two fertile eggs are laid; however, the first, the so-called alpha egg, is quite small and is usually quickly lost either to predators like skuas or sheathbills or to the constant shuffling

(Opposite)

Flowing head plumes are characteristic of all of the world's Eudtyptid, *or "erect-crested" penguins. The macaroni's name derives from a popular hair style, the one immortalized in the song "Yankee Doodle Dandy."* (RN)

Macaroni penguins nest in particularly steep locations, making it difficult for scientists to study their breeding biology, but affording remarkable vistas for those humans who wade through throngs of these "attack penguins" to gain their colonies' higher reaches. (RN)

and enormous chaos that envelop the colony. The second egg, the beta, is larger, and is the one generally brought to fruition. Both eggs may hatch, but rarely do two chicks survive. Sacrificing the alpha egg to the extant mayhem may be nature's way of preserving the species' numbers; another suggestion, focusing on evolutionary trends, is that macs and other crested penguins are moving toward single-egg clutches.

The generally steep slope presents other hazards. One day, my colleague Frank Todd and I were dropped by helicopter for our first-ever visit to one of the Welcome Islets in the Bay of Isles. The small islets rise like green and pink slags from the bay, the green from the abundant tussock, the pink from the rivers of guano created by the macs. The tussock is quite challenging because it often rises higher than five feet, and because its undercarriage is rutted with burrows of nocturnal blue petrels, diving petrels, and prions. One must also contend with the abundant skuas, nesting commonly and densely, and flourishing because of the night drop of thousands returning home. A helicopter provides an acceptable means for reaching the islets' higher elevations (the shores being too rocky for entry by zodiac), but it takes a while to traverse the green maze down to mac land.

There are acres upon acres of incubating, squawking tuft-heads. This particular day happened to be foggy and misty, and we had little expectation of sun to warm our bones or dry our clothes. Indeed, it looked like the penguins had endured days of sleet and rain: rivulets of brown water and molted feathers trickled everywhere, often collecting in large ponds at lower elevations. We split, Frank taking to the far eastern end of the islet, I planning to work south and west. After an hour of this gruel, conditions worsened: the mist turned to a steady rainfall, cameras and notepads had to be repacked, and as always seems to happen with worn gear and clothes, the icy drizzle found a path to bare skin. I was also caked from chest to boot-top, having slipped often in the mud and having spent much time prone, thrusting arms down burrows.

I raised my binoculars, trying to determine where Frank had wandered, just to keep the "buddy system" alive. A few hundred yards away stood his sodden, red-parka-clad figure, looking rather sullen. Noting my interest, he signaled disgust: first, both fingers pointing to his chest; then, his arms pumping up and down, fingers now gesticulating toward the mud; finally, he raised his right hand to his throat. A closer look revealed that he was totally covered in guano and molt, having made a close inspection of one of the rivulet-created ponds. It was little consolation to him that I, too, was thoroughly begrimed. We both knew that science meant dirty fingernails, and that creature comfort was relative. At least we'd gathered some interesting data: there were fewer macs than expected, leading, as usual, to more questions. Was this a bad year for krill, their predominant food? Had bad weather contributed? Had many failed breeders already departed?

By contrast, studying king penguins is physically easier because they usually avoid extreme slopes. They are found in more varying circumstances, some of which are surprising; for example, at Fortuna Glacier, the kings have colonized a relatively narrow bit of real estate between the 100–200-foot glacier wall and the correspondingly impressive nearby

I have often had the impression that, to penguins, man is just another penguin—different, less predictable, occasionally violent, but tolerable company when he sits still and minds his own business.

BERNARD STONEHOUSE
Penguins

Penguins are beautiful, interesting, and funny. They are a pleasure to watch even though they do smell and their voices are not melodious.

GEORGE GAYLORD SIMPSON
Penguins Past and Present,
Here and There

mountainside. The colony has increased to a few hundred pairs in a little more than a decade. They move to the higher elevations on the glacier to molt, leaving a dirty gray sheen on this magnificent piece of ice, which Shackleton partially traversed on his overland trek to Stromness.

Kings are the monarchs of the subantarctic rim: the world's second largest penguins, standing 3½ feet tall, weighing up to seventy-five pounds, glowing with inverted, orange-yellow comma marks on the sides of their heads and a smattering of gray through the black back feathering; their underbellies and throats are immaculately white.

My first experience with them was at the famous Salisbury Plain rookery on the island's north side, in the Bay of Isles. This is the location where Robert Cushman Murphy did much pioneering ornithological work in 1912–13, and where notables such as Niall Rankin, Harrison Matthews, and Brian Roberts also practiced. Broad glaciers descend to the bay and huge peaks tower to the south, lending a majestic presence to the 12,000 or so pairs of kings nestled on and immediately below the plain's tussock hillside. The weather, as usual, shifts from minute to minute. The best entry, assuming a calm sea, is by zodiac landing on the broad expanse of cobble beach, which opens northward into the bay. The colony requires a half-mile southward traipse over the boggy grass and smaller tussock clumps to the rising hillside. The beautiful Grace Glacier (named after Murphy's wife) dominates to starboard.

At the beach, the visitor is usually met by one or a few of the local tour guides, some nattily attired characters who look like they've just returned from either a feeding run offshore or a casting call at a Madison Avenue ad agency. The invitation is compelling: the welcome committee (I've had up to twelve kings leading me in this fashion) rushes to your feet, inspects your footwear, nods, calls hoarsely and then, in unison, turns backs and starts waddling south toward the main colony. They often look back to make sure that you're following; if not, they stop, turn on their heels and stare, seemingly asking why you're moving so slowly. (If you have the temerity to lie prone, they're apt to climb on top of you and start poking around until you're convinced to move!) Kings are extremely confident of their carriage; when they do happen to trip or stumble, the offending rock or clump of grass is given a long, menacing glance that assigns blame for the misstep. Resuming their pace with heads cocked to the sky, they exude an effete snobbery that no other penguin can claim.

During the subantarctic summer, Salisbury Plain is a muddy, wet pasture. Abundant glacier melt and rainfall contribute substantially to the conditions. After just a few hundred yards, both welcome committee

A pair of macaroni penguins offers a greeting from the tussock mound nest site at the Welcome Islets of South Georgia. The friendly gesture belies the feisty and irritable disposition of these birds. (RN)

and guest are waddling severely in the muck, the kings definitely having the easier time of it. Approaching the tussock clumps, a few South Georgian teals fly by, uttering their characteristic "pink, pink" chirps. From this closer distance, calls and peels from the kings are more readily detected. The sexes have similar hoarse, wailing cries, the females' call, to my ears, being slightly higher-pitched and having a slightly faster delivery rate. The wails are interrupted by piercing whistles, which emanate from fat, brown, woolly-bear creatures that look like stuffed Christmas dolls, not penguins. These are the so-called "oakum boys" (or girls)—in reality, baby kings just a few months in age, soon to emerge from behind their disguises as bona fide, albeit pale, versions of their elders. The woolly-like feathering protects oakums from the rigors of the harsh South Georgian weather, but seems more perfectly designed to humor us anthropomorphic observers.

"Oakum" refers to the brown, stringy caulking material that old sealers and whalers used to waterproof their casks and barrels. Murphy joked that the oakums reminded him of college boys rushing from class to class. The comedy continues as the young birds start molting out of their wool, the emergence usually proceeding from the ankles upwards. The woolly feathers start to drop in patches, but not necessarily in any order, often leaving the youngsters in an even more risible state than before. The woolly feathering is so protective that if the sun begins to shine the youngsters' panting increases noticeably. The danger is that they'll try swimming before the postnatal molt is completed; if the woolly protectant is severely dampened, the oakums won't be able to retain warmth as readily, and they may perish.

The breeding cycle is curious. Unlike their larger relatives, the emperor penguins, kings don't raise their young annually, but rather in two out of every three years. In high summer a colony might reveal all stages of the kings' life history: courting and copulating adults; incubating adults; adult changeovers (both male and female share incubation of the single egg, which rests on the tops of the feet and is covered by the bird's brood patch); scraggly birds that have just finished breeding; non- or failed breeders; recently molted and returned adults; oakums in various stages of woolliness; hatching, naked chicks; and, perhaps, even the laying of eggs. Each colony adheres to a different schedule, and each life history stage is likely to be found in differing percentages.

As one approaches the Salisbury Plain hillside, the noise increases markedly; soon one is enveloped in a huge mass of incubating adults, at the foot of the rising slope and above. The colony appears to be expanding, stretching farther onto the plain and closer to the bay. In totality, it forms a great amphitheater, a Hollywood Bowl of king penguins. Tiptoeing upward through the throng, a few newborns may be seen emerging from their parents' brood patches. The world's southernmost breeding land bird, the South Georgia pipit, makes an appearance, flitting back and forth from one tussock clump to another. Well above the pit, at the colony's apex, a pastoral fantasy dances across the plain: layers of green and brown juxtaposed against the white of Grace Glacier and the occasional blue of the sky; orange penguin flecks popping through long strands of green tussock; the fog moving like a respirator, increasing and decreasing with the changing, swirling wind.

A rockhopper penguin from the Falklands shows off its characteristic Eudyptid *hairdo. There are many islands just north of the true Antarctic fringe that share some of the same wildlife as the Deep South, or which possess some close relatives of their Antarctic congeners.* (RN)

At the edge of the kings, below, an immediately resident pair of brown skuas, the hawklike gull predators of The Ice, scream hoarsely and tend to the needs of their brown beggar children. There are frequent clashes with passing stray skuas that mistakenly enter the protected area of this one pair. The resulting aerial pursuits, with frequent wingovers, dodges, and twists, play out over the dense slope of the king colony. Soon the avenger returns home to its mate, the pair greeting each other with strident long calls and the customary spreading of wings, showing off their white primary patches.

These sultans of avian s.w.a.t. are particular favorites, in my mind providing perfect metaphors for the life-and-death struggles that reign so obviously here. Skuas have a bad reputation, which is unfortunate, because they perform the important biological function of culling the weak, unprotected, and sick. It is one incredible feat to beak and to fly away with a heavy king penguin egg. An entire chick, however, is more difficult; in this instance, skuas work in tandem, stretching, pulling, and mangling a collected item until it is reduced to more manageable morsels. Skuas are fiercely protective of their turf, especially with young just hatched, and claw marks may be a lingering souvenir for the working scientist. It is said that skuas can be distracted by holding a stick or fist above one's head. However, I've had a marauding skua knock a three-foot-long two-by-four right out of my hands, surprising both of us but causing permanent damage to neither. Murphy, too, was a staunch admirer of these dive-bombing hellions:

*I became extremely well acquainted with the Brown Skua, which has left, I believe, a more vivid impression in my memory than any other bird I have met. The skuas look and act like miniature eagles. They fear nothing, never seek to avoid being conspicuous, and, by every token of behavior, they are lords of the far south. In effect, they are gulls which have turned into hawks. Not only are they the enemies of every creature they can master, living almost entirely by ravin and slaughter, but they also have the appearance of a bird of prey in the general color of their plumage, the pointed, erectile hackles on the neck, the hooked bill, and the long, sharp, curved claws, which seem incongruous on webbed feet. They are tremendously strong, heavy, and vital birds which, in the air, look massive rather than speedy. It is therefore somewhat surprising to learn that they can overtake in free flight such swift, long-winged petrels as the Shoe-maker (*Procellaria aequinoctialis). *Energy is apparent in every movement of the skua—in its rapacity, in the quantity of food it can ingest within a few moments, and in the volume and continuousness of the screams that issue from its throat. . . . One usually thinks of the skuas' voice as a scream, because they make their most vivid picture when they stand in angry or defiant attitude, their*

A brown skua poses against the green moss background of its Nelson Island home in the Antarctic Peninsula. The Wild Ice possesses two skua species, both of which are adept at scavenging. Brown skua pairs not only carve out a territory of their own for breeding; with other brown skua pairs in the neighborhood they divide nearby penguin colonies for predation purposes. Where both species are found, the south polar skua spends much more time foraging at sea. (RN)

wings held upright in a posture of those on ancient Norse helmets, and protest with ear-splitting cries.

In preparing scores of king penguin specimens on Salisbury's beach, Murphy found skuas to be diligent lab assistants, patiently

cleaning the fat from the inside of the penguin skins. When the latter, turned inside out, were placed before them, the skuas would pick off the blubber as cleanly as it could have been done with a scraper, and in much less time. They would snip off small bits with the hooks of their beaks, swallowing one after another about as rapidly as a chicken picks up strewn corn. On one occasion I had thirty-five skuas ready to work, each attempting to perform on my behalf this fundamental taxonomic process! My helpers battled unendingly, however, even when there was ample room for all, and one or sometimes two old champions monopolized each penguin skin most of the time, to the detriment of efficiency. In fighting, they raised their white-marked wings, and jumped at each other like game cocks, except that they did not use their claws. They knocked each other down in jolly fashion, and pulled out feathers, the battles being half on the ground and half in air. The victor always raised its wings and screamed before turning again toward the banquet and driving off the birds which had slipped into its place.

One of the great glories of ornithology is an intimate knowledge of your subject, which usually increases to a level of unfettered admiration. It is a bond between species, a relationship that only the researcher who has endured the travails of inquiry can appreciate. Indeed, Murphy developed a healthy affection for these Huns:

Skuas are the berserkers among birds. They seem to have a diabolical gift to be a scourge. . . . But in spite of their voracity, rapine, and cannibalism, the skuas quickly make themselves the beneficiaries of a peculiar, sentimental, anthropomorphic interest. When they crowd around you, and look up with bright, fearless, unsuspicious brown eyes, accept the bounty you offer them, and show no more concern over the loudest shouts, whistles, or handclaps than if they were stone-deaf, you succumb to their charm, and subscribe to the principle that their supremacy of might must be deserved.

Such symbioses are enacted throughout South Georgia: at St. Andrew's and Royal bays, Fortuna Glacier, Hercules Point, Paul Beach, Gold Harbor, and elsewhere. Penguins exploit whatever turf they can to accommodate their large numbers; skuas patrol the edges as the vaunted knights of population dynamics; albatrosses connect the airspace between heaven and earth. At times there is simply too much for the human visitor to observe, too much to examine, too much with which to commune. In other words, biological overload. Choices are dictated by limited amounts of time and complicated by fears of missing something. My solution to this predicament, however, has led to a supremely obvious decision: to opt for as much time as possible with the big albatrosses.

Why? Because, above all, I am a seabirder. I confess to being absolutely gripped by the skill of these black-belt aeronauts, captivated by their mastery of a domain in which I am so totally incompetent. We humans live and work on the 25 percent of our planet that is land; albatrosses, by necessity, must come to land to breed, but most of their lives are spent over water, that 75 percent of the earth that to them is comfortable but to us is alien. Often I've tried imagining myself in their cosmos, soaring beyond the mountains and cliffs to career over rough seas with the greatest of ease, skillfully coping with the harshest of elements. But my bones are too heavy, and my arms and legs misshapen; I've evolved for another kind of existence. Admiring their design and skill, we might ask who more fittingly represents the "higher" species. This speculation suggests a partnership; knowing more about them and their lives enriches our outlook, enriches me. It becomes a higher form of inquiry.

That inquiry starts at sea. All seabirders remember their first trip to the Deep South. Mine was intense, optimistic, and cold: hours after long hours spent on the fantail, scanning the horizon and sea, just waiting and praying for my quarry to appear. My day of triumph proved rather forbidding. There was a dark overcast, the sun only rarely streaking through. It definitely was an albatross kind of a day, with a strong thirty- to forty-knot wind blowing the swell into white spindrifts, the ship rolling a good 15 degrees as we headed south across the Drake Passage. True to form, the seabirds were having no problems maneuvering, flying in and out of the fast-moving fog. Finally, an albatross appeared from out of absolutely nowhere, rising quickly and closing much faster than I had expected. I can't do better than Murphy in describing such an otherworldly moment:

Near by . . . flew the long-anticipated fowl, even more majestic, more supreme in its element, than my imagination had pictured. . . . They would fly again and again across the quarterdeck, jerking up their heads like spirited steeds and showing curiosity and temptation in every action. Sometimes they wiggled their feet in air with an amusing running motion, or spread their translucent webs so that they looked blood-red against the sky. Sometimes they halted so abruptly in flight that it seemed they had struck an invisible barrier. During brisk breezes they zoomed across the stern close enough for me to see the color of their eyes and to hear the humming swish of their stiff quills . . . I now belong to a higher cult of mortals, for I have seen the albatross!

My inquiry then continued at the nesting grounds, some lonely and inaccessible stages where these actors and actresses play to disinterested audiences of avian neighbors. There are fourteen albatross species worldwide: the largest is the wandering, with a thirteen-foot wingspan; the smallest, the sleek light-mantled sooty, with a seven-foot span. High, windy promontories or island tops are preferred nest locations because they allow easy takeoffs; albatrosses clearly choose rooms with great views. They are faithful to these sites, returning time after time to the same nesting mound, and they generally remain faithful to a single mate for life. They are quite long-lived, perhaps to sixty years or more in the case of wanderers and royals. After returning from postbreeding vacations at sea, albatrosses engage in dynamic courtship rituals, embellished with much strutting, swaying, bowing, honking, and grunting. Some of this is compelling; during the wanderers' routine, both birds may stretch their beaks to the sky, extending wings to the maximum, breasts nearly locking in an affirmation that another breeding season has begun.

An albatross's power and agility in flight give little indication of its supreme gentility on land. Whereas the act of assessing an egg's presence is a dangerous proposition in mac land, with albatrosses there's the contrast of their foot-long, massive beaks gently nuzzling and nibbling one's outstretched, inquisitive arms. The cordiality may reflect the albatrosses' huge investment in these eggs; with wanderers, incubation and fledging of chicks is extremely lengthy, taking up to 280 days, which confines adults to a schedule of raising young in two out of every three years. Young wanderers, after finally leaving their elevated nurseries, circle the Southern Ocean for up to eight years before returning to make their first attempts at breeding.

South Georgia is blessed with many breeding albatrosses: black-browed, gray-headed, wandering, and light-mantled sooty, the last being the only one whose breeding biology had eluded my sustained exami-

(Opposite)

A medium-sized albatross of the subantarctic fringe, this gray-headed albatross casts a determined stare from its tussock-surrounded nest site on Diego Ramirez island, southwest of Cape Horn in the Drake Passage. (RN)

The great hurrah about wild animals is that they exist at all, and the greater hurrah is the actual moment of seeing them. Because they have a nice dignity, and prefer to have nothing to do with me, not even as the simple objects of my vision. They show me by their very wariness what a prize it is simply to open my eyes and behold.

ANNIE DILLARD
Pilgrim at Tinker Creek

With chest fully inflated and bill pointed to the sky, this wandering albatross announces its return to its nest site on Prion Island, South Georgia. (RN)

On Prion Island, South Georgia, this wanderer extends its wings as the wind comes up around midday. Albatrosses clearly choose "rooms with a view," some of the most picturesque breeding sites in the avian world. (RN)

Above: The royal albatross is the wanderer's closest relative, nesting on the New Zealand side of the Wild Ice. This couple is nesting on Campbell Island.
Left: The investment of adult royal albatrosses in their chicks is enormous. This emerging youngster will have about nine months to go before fledging. (CM)

Wandering albatross courtship is punctuated with numerous bows, dances, struts, and gapes. After the breeding season, the mates head to sea, but not together, generally to feed and to replenish their energy. On the headlands where they nest—here, Prion Island, a small islet on the north coast of South Georgia—each returning bird must run a gauntlet of adults awaiting the return of their mates. (RN)

The wandering is the largest of the world's albatrosses, with a wingspan of up to thirteen feet. Coming to shore only to breed, albatrosses are masters of that 75 percent of the earth's surface that we humans find so alien. The Drake Passage, where this wanderer was photographed, is a favored foraging area for many species of albatrosses, attracted not only by the potential for food, but by the howling winds. Ornithologist Robert Cushman Murphy said that albatrosses were the birds that caused the wind to blow. (RN)

The courtship display of the wandering albatross is a particularly appealing spectacle. Since the fledging of their last chick, this pair has roamed far and wide over the Southern Ocean—not together—before returning to their favored nest site on lonely Albatross Island in South Georgia. (RN)

White-chinned petrel. (RN)

Imperial shag. (TDR)

Light-mantled sooty albatross. (TDR)

Fuzzy chick of the king penguin. (MJ)

Brown skuas are the vaunted knights of population dynamics in the Wild Ice, patrolling the beaches and penguin colonies for the weak, infirm, and unawares. Their biological pruning often goes unappreciated by anthropomorphics. On "Minerva Alarm" Islet, South Georgia, as elsewhere, skuas are highly protective of their turf and young, boldly displaying their white wing patches at any hint of disruption. (RN)

There are many children of the Wild Ice. This southern giant petrel parent and chick pose amid their tussock-crowded home on Albatross Island, South Georgia. (RN)

nation. It is a beautiful, graceful, and mysterious specimen, witness Murphy:

The Antarctic Sooty Albatross, with its pearly body contrasting with the dark cap and wings [gives] it the fanciful appearance of a cowled monk. . . . Most of the bird's vernacular names, such as "Piew" and "Pee-arr," are taken from its peculiar call at the breeding grounds. . . . Their white-ringed eyes, which gave them a sort of perpetually astonished expression, were conspicuous even at ship's lengths. No doubt these queer orbital marks, together with the somber guise of the fowl, have been responsible both for the name Phoebetria, *the "prophet," and for the legendary place that the Sooty Albatross seems to hold among seafarers.*

I'd often seen them riding the drafts up and down the faces of huge tabular icebergs, well to the south of their Convergence breeding cliffs, and I'd encountered them in the Drake, competing evenly with many of their albatross congeners. But I'd only managed brief glimpses during the peak of their courtship on South Georgia's rocky cliffs. Their allure increased exponentially, as more years and visits produced fewer satisfying encounters.

From British Antarctic Survey research, we know that light-mantled sooties are biennial nesters, feeding primarily on squid and, to a lesser extent, krill (fish also may be taken). They roam long distances—often as far south as the pack ice—in search of a meal. Relatively infrequent chick feedings and a less-energizing dominant food item (squid contains less calcium than krill) contribute to a fledging period that reaches 140 days and, ultimately, to the nonannual breeding schedule. The birds prefer nesting solitarily on the highest cliffs and ridges, although occasionally a few pairs may nest closely together.

Their lamenting, two-syllabled calls have been compared to the meows of cats and the brays of donkeys. They call most actively before egg laying, but will continue for a short while into their seventy days of incubation. In Harrison Matthews's words:

At the nesting season a loud shrill cry is produced. One pair was found at the nest before the egg was laid. The female sat on the nest while the male stood on the ledge near by, frequently uttering this cry. It consists of two notes, first a loud shrill one made with the beak open and the head thrown back, so that the bird is looking straight up into the sky. This is an expiratory note and is immediately followed by a much lower and quieter inspiratory note, made with the bill closed and held pointing down to the ground so that the under surface of the mandible rests against the breast. Every two or three times the male did this the female stood up on the nest and answered in the same way and then sat down again.

Given an unparalleled chance to fill my light-mantled sooty gap, I enthusiastically approached the late 1988 field season at South Georgia. Frank Todd and I were working aboard the British ice patrol ship *Endurance,* named, of course, after Shackleton's ship crushed in the Weddell Sea more than seventy years ago. With the generous assistance of Captain Tom Sunter and the British Royal Navy, we were collaborating on the British Antarctic Survey's long-term study of South Georgian penguin colonies and seabird stacks. It was a special opportunity to rely on the ship's helicopters—the Lynxes—to visit places that hadn't yet been studied in depth. Many of the offshore stacks were impossible to climb, for example, even if scientists could be off-loaded by zodiacs on the riotous shorelines. There were many questions to explore: Which birds were breeding? Were they on eggs or with young? Was there rat infestation or not? Of particular note, we were trying to determine whether the blue petrel, a recently discovered breeding species, could be found in new locations. Another focus was the spread of the island's king penguins; we would have the opportunity to census almost simultaneously a large number of colonies and to update the latest reports and studies. Best of all, we knew that at least four of our study sites had light-mantled sooty nests; if courting birds quickly divulged themselves as we arrived, we'd likely have some special moments.

After some good finds—blue petrel remains at the R-32 stack on the southeastern side of the island and the notable increase of kings at Fortuna—our appointed day at Royal Bay arrived. Located far down on the island's southeastern end, it opens broadly northeast toward the sea, exposing it dearly to the prevailing winds. A few small harbors exist, but protection from the wind is minimal and anchorages don't hold. There are hordes of kings, a few substantial mac colonies lining the eastern cliffs, a few gentoo penguin colonies to the west, and occasionally, when the bay is calm, spouting right whales. Our copter trip into Royal Bay offered spectacular views of the Ross Glacier to the west and the titanic Weddell Glacier at the bay's mouth to the east, the latter fronted by the enormous Will Point king penguin colony. We landed at the base of some towering, almost vertical cliffs, slightly northwest of the Weddell Glacier and adjacent to a scenic rounded spit that prevented some of the glacial melt from reaching the bay. Frank scurried off to the penguins on the spit while I quickly became mesmerized by the calling light-mantled sooties.

After crossing through the narrow pass and veering upward, I found myself marooned, as already described, 200 feet above the tussock plain, having misjudged the seemingly easy path to the albatrosses.

My predicament had continued for many nervous moments when an unexpected silence ensued. The "p'yarrr–eees" had abated. I was beyond earshot of the kings below, and the wind curiously lapsed, accentuating the meltwater trickling down the slope past my hands and the precarious foothold that mired me, face-in, to the slope. Swiveling my head carefully to the west, I could see the outlines of Moltke Harbor, where I'd enjoyed the training battles of young bull elephant seals and the sight of Arctic terns returning after their long, 7,500-mile journey from the far north. It was also where I'd first climbed after light-mantled sooty nests.

I was jolted from reverie by a light-mantled sooty that whizzed by at topflight speed, almost eyeball to eyeball, heading swiftly toward Wed-

This light-mantled sooty albatross begins its "p'yarrr–eee" call by sky-pointing in the tussock high above St. Andrew's Bay, South Georgia. The call is induced by the passing mate, other sooties flying by being totally ignored. (RN)

(Overleaf)

A light-mantled sooty albatross overlooks its kingdom from the heights of St. Andrew's Bay in South Georgia. It shares its realm with tens of thousands of king penguins on the two-mile-long nesting beach below, with many elephant seals wallowing in the muck at the base of the breeding cliffs. (RN)

After returning to its cliff-side throne high above Royal Bay, South Georgia, a light-mantled sooty albatross snuggles and allopreens with its mate. Light-mantled sooties are the smallest of the world's albatrosses, raising one chick every two years and feeding on squid and fish. (RN)

dell Glacier. There wasn't the slightest hesitation or change of direction as the gray beauty zipped along, just a few feet out. I easily discerned its beautiful white half-eye ring and the blue sulcus line on the bill, and almost touched its sleek, pointed wings as I carefully turned to follow its flight. Fifty yards beyond, it banked sharply north and started looping back in a counterclockwise arc. Vigorous "p'yarrr–eees, p'yarrr–eees" suddenly resumed to my side. The arcing albatross altered course, plummeting directly toward me and the nearby voice, veering slightly right before braking wings, lifting legs, and disappearing no more than a few arm's lengths around the corner. I can't remember the tussock holds or finding any newly discovered indentations in the slope, nor do I recall the details of the careening, thrusting maneuver that must have transpired. Quite unexpectedly, though, I was seated next to a pair of nesting light-mantled sooties. Finally, my prize. I hardly noticed the blood returning to my insensate, shaking legs; I'd moved from precipice to throne, a view that now encompassed Royal Bay's far western reaches, the vast panorama of tussock and thousands of kings below, and a dramatic expanse of whitecaps to the northeast. The downward path that fortuitously appeared to the west (now on my left) hardly registered.

Out came my notebook. The sitting bird, in a slightly elevated nest mound, continued to call, beak extended toward its mate. The routine was familiar: beak extended high for the exhaled "p'yarrr" portion of the call, then dropped as low as possible during the inhaled, wheezing "eee." The standing bird repeated the entreaty with gusto, its beak shaking and its neck quivering on the inspiratory second syllable. The two started nuzzling, neck to neck, before proceeding to a short bout of beak fencing and some mutual feather preening. Finally they changed over, revealing the single egg below. The new incubator shuffled and wiggled to get comfortable, inhaled noticeably, then began preening itself. It stopped to grab some rooted strands of tussock in its mandibles, coursing the green plumes from root to tip. It housecleaned some, moving dirt, moss, and sticks to tidy its place.

I stopped writing as the newly relieved mate slowly approached me—a tousled, filthy hallucination sharing its ledge. Up-and-down head movements were the first gesture, followed by a side-to-side strut that put me within pecking distance. Next its beak bolted skyward with an accompaniment of quiet cooing sounds before it lowered its head slowly to wipe its bill on my forearm. Assured, it stood still and our eyes met directly. Transfixed, I could not turn away.

Neither of us retreated, and for long minutes the contest continued. In the bird's eyes I saw and felt glory, life's efflorescence in earth's last pristine wilderness. Their luster reflected the whole ebb and flow of time in the Wild Ice: the cold brutality of the Antarctic winter; the easing toward spring, each day bequeathing fresh harbingers of a new season about to flourish; long, glowing streaks reemerging in the morning and evening skies; loud cracks and groans of shifting ice; penguins refueling and fattening their chubby bodies; compacted breeding seasons and erupting cohorts of newly emerged chicks and pups; speedy retreats before the rehardening of winter.

My compatriot was a permanent character in this unyielding drama, sharing the sky above and the water below but jeopardizing neither. I couldn't discern its interest in the meaning of life or the design and purpose of the universe, but perhaps these are irrelevancies to an albatross. I savored its fragility and gentleness; I embraced its wealth. But what did this albatross see in *my* eyes? Did it see a fellow traveler relishing these wild encounters, or an ignoble species disposed to consume and to dominate? What pact had this human made?

I don't know what answers it perceived, nor whether they mattered. However satisfied or discouraged, the light-mantled sooty flew off and headed east, leaving me with the weight of ages and a numbing chill. Dazed, I slinked onto the downward path, head lowered to find the holds, still trying to shake my emotions. Craning upward for a last glance at the ledge, I noticed in the distance that my winged partner was returning, circling around for one more pass. As it neared, our eyes met again and held. The prophet dipped its right wing, nodded, then departed into a life I'd only begun to imagine.

Into the eyes of light-mantled sooty albatrosses we gaze. What do they see in our eyes? Are we their brothers and sisters, sharing the sky above and the water below and disturbing neither, or consumers who disregard our fellow travelers on this planet? (RN)

(Overleaf)

The long days of spring and summer in the Antarctic region offer a panoply of colors, moods, and forms. Sunset and sunrise are particularly appealing, lending an otherworldly softness to the surroundings. On this evening in the Lemaire Channel, the musical tinkling of ice was accompanied by a sudden drop in wind, imparting a stillness that could be breathed, almost touched. (RN)

M A R K   J O N E S

Flow of Ice, Ebbs of Time

A Journey through the Cycle of Ice in the Southern Ocean

With regal splendor the blue berg beckoned from the horizon. Glowing. Intricate. Its motion was almost stately as it defied the elements. Defied comprehension. Fluted, pitted, and crevassed, hollowed, gouged, and sculpted, the convoluted spires and chasms appeared to emit their own surreal hues of light. Intense dark blue light of almost indigo depth emanated from its every cavity, enhanced by a surface glazing of white frost and set against the backdrop of a leaden sky heavy with the power of an imminent storm.

Muffled against the rising wind, I stood transfixed as the ice drew closer, its details coming into focus with ever-increasing complexity and grace. Petrels wheeled round and round before the blue faces, riding the wind eddies deflected by its polished angles, their black-and-white wings flashing. On a smaller slab of ice in the lee of the big berg, a flock of penguins sat preening meticulously. Above all, the blue berg commanded attention, lending a touch of fantasy to the otherwise simple Antarctic seascape. Waves seemed to beat indignantly at its sides, stopping abruptly in their relentless wanderings, funneling into the berg's very heart through deep caverns and grottoes, and streaming from its flanks in great foaming cascades.

Where in the vast reaches of the Antarctic had it come from? Scrutinizing the towers, pinnacles, tunnels, and arches, and their overwhelming color, I tried to read the blue berg's story, attempting to visualize the odyssey etched into its every detail, while I remained engrossed in the spectacle of its entirety. Though common types and forms of icebergs do recur, this one was unique, unlike any I had heard of or seen. Its complicated shapes imparted an ancient appearance. Such a deep blue is indeed characteristic of old ice, ice that has been compressed beneath many other vast layers; ice that has over a tremendous period of time had all the air squeezed from between its molecules. Dense ice. Ice like this can be found at the bases of the largest, slow-moving glaciers that wend their

(Opposite)

The action of wind and waves can sculpt chunks of ice into amazing shapes. Often these segments will be blown against the shore and subsequently stranded by the receding tide. There they melt at a much faster rate, since their every hollow is exposed to the wind and the sun dancing on the delicate contours. (MJ)

way from the polar ice cap into the ocean, great chunks occasionally breaking off the leading edges to become free icebergs. At the mercy of wind and waves a berg may become eroded, crafted by the forces of nature, sculpted into shapes not even the most whimsical artist could imagine. The blue berg was one of these, and maybe this was its tale. For how many seasons had it lingered, traveling the ocean currents, gradually being drawn away from the continent where it was born? How many more years would it survive? At that moment I had no idea of the pertinence of my questions.

Slowly, ever so slowly, the berg began to roll. Almost imperceptibly it leaned, unbalanced perhaps by the large swells and searching for a new equilibrium, almost as if pondering the consequences of its actions. Great cataracts of water poured from once-submerged canyons, while delicate pillars were thrust beneath the roiling waves. Then, hesitantly, seemingly trying to undo its mistake, it began to bob back upright. The stresses must have been phenomenal, too much to bear for the simple ice crystals so long bonded together. Portions began to break off, first on one side then the other, crashing into the sea. The blue berg heaved this way and that as more chunks tumbled with tremendous groans, loud booms, and resounding splashes. Unseen shockwaves echoed through its azure valleys, causing millions of hairline fissures to spread and cleave the ice apart. Huge blocks sheared, letting the ocean flood in and causing the berg's very heart to crumble. And crumble it did; within minutes it was all over. The blue berg no longer heaved over the huge Southern Ocean swells, rebuffing the wind and waves that had for countless attempts buffeted its flanks. Now those same waves rolled on, barely jostling its diminishing remnants.

The storm retreated, without having carried out its threat. Tearing a rent in the cloud canopy, the setting sun danced its last rays upon the fast dispersing ice shards. The petrels departed in search of new air currents on which to glide. The penguins on their floe, having rode out the frantic bobbing, resumed their preening. The ship turned southward, heading deeper into the Antarctic, while I turned up my collar and, peering toward the horizon, pondered the empty seascape stretched out ahead.

Antarctica is a separate world, a realm of complicated simplicity. One can feel its presence in the approaches, sailing south from more

A typical overcast Antarctic day casts gentle light on gentoos and bergs at Couverville Island. (TDR)

temperate climes: a growing emptiness as the cold becomes more intense, life appearing gradually less varied yet increasingly abundant. A sense of freedom is borne on the unsullied wind, which never touches land as it drives the seas forever eastward in a succession of stunning calms and raging storms. Standing on deck, one may follow the reeling albatross, feel the drop in temperature, the bite of the wind, and the motion of the waves. Yet it is the presence of ice, from the first occasional fragments, escalating in shape, form, and frequency, and finally dominating all else, that brings the assurance of arrival in Antarctica.

The first view of Antarctica is always an iceberg. It may be a monolith hovering on the horizon, a barely discernible specter looming out of the mist, or perhaps a sun-spangled, dazzling icon marking the gateway to this new world. It will undoubtedly be icebergs that leave the most lasting impressions on the imagination of visitors. Some may see a castle with fortified ramparts, others a cathedral with towering spire or just a flat-topped city block. For many it is impossible to disassociate the fantastic proportions of icebergs from the familiar shapes of civilization. But in the purity of the Antarctic setting, icebergs remain simply icebergs, naturally awe-inspiring, with infinite free forms to play the light and appeal to a viewer's aesthetics. They are also transient, dying bodies, melting by the minute, leaving the continent that created them, ending the same way as they began—as drops of water in the vast body of the ocean.

The World of Ice

Antarctica is a land of superlatives. The fifth largest continent, it is also the highest, the driest, the coldest, and the windiest, features that can be explained with one simple household word: ice. Earth has been dubbed "the water planet," yet 99 percent of the world's fresh water is in solid mineral state. Representing the purest form of water, and covering about one-tenth of the globé, some 90 percent of this ice is in the Antarctic, making up its vast polar ice cap.

Without its ice cap the continent would in fact be the smallest, a much reduced landmass in the east and barely a string of islands and archipelagoes in the west. The ice merges it together. During the winter, with the freezing of the surrounding seas, the area of Antarctica effectively doubles to more than 30 million square kilometers, making it well over three times as large as the United States, or about the size of Africa. Its highest mountain, the Vinson Massif, peaks at only 5,140 meters,

Approaching Antarctica from the tip of South America across the awesome Drake Passage, it doesn't take long for the temperatures to drop as you sail through the Antarctic Convergence. A giant berg, looking like a ghostly aircraft carrier, will soon loom out of the fog. This flat-topped monolith may be glassy smooth or split and fissured by wave and wind action, radiating hues from bottle green to the iridescent blue of a kingfisher. (CM)

Parts of the Antarctic have been swept by winds recorded at 200 miles per hour, and the usual weather forecast calls for high gusts and blows. Yet there are occasional moments when the tranquillity of the Wild Ice belies the violent nature of the environment. (RN)

(Overleaf)

The Antarctic Peninsula is studded with high alpine peaks and deeply crevassed glaciers, making overland travel on this part of the continent both difficult and dangerous. The British Antarctic Survey base Faraday is only a few kilometers away from where this photograph was taken at the southern end of Lemaire Channel. (CM)

The land retains an identity of its own, still deeper and more subtle than we can know. Our obligation towards it then becomes simple: to approach with an uncalculating mind, with an attitude of regard.

BARRY LOPEZ
Arctic Dreams

moderate by world standards, yet the majority of the Antarctic mountain chains are smothered by the tremendous overlaying ice of the polar plateau. In places the thickness of this ice cap reaches 4,700 meters, masking not only mountains but filling deep trenches that would otherwise lie below sea level, and giving the continent an average elevation of about four kilometers. It is on this high polar plateau, with the ice acting as a huge heat sink, its surface effectively reflecting back 80 percent of the sun's radiation, that the coldest temperatures on earth have been recorded at minus 89 degrees centigrade. Winter averages here are regularly in the region of minus 50 to minus 60 degrees centigrade, with summer highs around minus 15 degrees centigrade.

The cold is so intense that it allows absolutely no free moisture, even with the vast amount of water locked in the ice cap. A kind of dew does form, but only as miniature ice crystals called diamond dust. Snow is so powder-dry that it squeaks like styrofoam under every step. The equivalent precipitation of snowfall over much of the continent is less than five centimeters per year, making it one of the earth's driest deserts. It is here also that the strongest winds are generated, driving phenomenal blizzards. Termed katabatic winds, these are gravity-induced by the ice itself, the result of supercooled, dense air rolling down unimpeded from the higher reaches of the polar plateau, gathering momentum as it nears the coast. Here wind speeds can peak at nearly 320 kilometers per hour, and in the coastal regions of Terre Adélie that receive the full force of these katabatics, the daily average over a four-year period exceeded 66 kilometers per hour. As these cold winds meet the relatively warmer maritime air, localized blizzards and dense fog can be produced.

On a larger scale, the cold air masses generated by the ice cap react with the warmer westerly winds moving over the ocean to create a vicious storm belt surrounding Antarctica. Massive cyclonic depression systems are constantly being formed, spiraling toward the continent, dissipating their energies on the coastlines and surrounding ocean, and establishing a permanent ring of low pressure known as the Antarctic Trough. At any one time there may be a half dozen or more fronts closing in on the continent, causing some of the roughest seas imaginable. These are the latitudes known to mariners as the "roaring forties," the "furious fifties," and the "screaming sixties." Some of the larger storms may occasionally reach up onto the polar plateau itself, causing blizzards and snowfalls far in the interior before the system finally decays.

Whatever the statistics, ice constitutes the foundation upon which all of Antarctica is based. Ice is Antarctica and Antarctica is ice, it is the be-all and end-all of the environment. About 1 percent of the continent is ice-free. No one and nothing evades it, and therefore nothing exists without it.

Ice comes in infinite shapes and varieties, from the smallest spicule to the largest glacier. Over seventy-eight types have been specifically named: from pancake ice to bullet ice, green ice to grease ice, ice dust to ice flowers, ice haycocks to ice saddles. Ice can be grounded or it can float, it can be fast or it can rumple, it can form tongues or it can form fringes. Ice can be anything; in Antarctica ice *is* everything.

Light slips through to distant peaks in this late sunset view of the Lemaire Channel. The great American explorer and geologist Larry Gould remarked that Antarctic light often evokes the "feeling of jazz." (RN)

(Overleaf)

Under the darkening clouds of an imminent storm, a surreal light is cast upon the smooth waterworn contours of a turned iceberg that serves as a convenient resting place for a small band of chinstrap penguins. (MJ)

Evening sun glints through an eroded berg in the Bellingshausen Sea. Over two summers in 1819–21, the Russian explorer Bellingshausen circumnavigated Antarctica well to the south of Captain Cook. He discovered such major chunks of land as Alexander Island, thought then to be part of the mainland. This sighting forms the basis for the Russian claim to be the discoverers of the Antarctic continent. (CM)

(Opposite)

An impressive panorama of clouds and mountains stretches out near Anvers Island. (TDR)

We are trying to say that environmentally sensitive development is an oxymoron when it comes to pristine wilderness.

TIM MAHONEY
quoted in the Washington Post

An Ocean of Life

All that lives in Antarctica has evolved in accordance with the qualities of ice, from the seals that in winter spend months submerged in subzero water below the sea ice, breathing through cracks but rarely hauling out onto floes, to the lichens clinging tenaciously to a few exposed rocks as close as 400 kilometers to the pole, surviving the long polar night while frozen solid and caked in snow and ice.

Some algae have perfected their association with ice even further. The minute snow algae actually grow on the open snow fields, tinting the sweeping white landscapes in delicate greens and pinks. One particular species, appropriately named the ice algae, has developed a special technique. When the ocean freezes over, seawater seeps between the layers of solid ice and accumulated snow, carrying with it the microscopic ice algae. Here they begin to grow, lying dormant through the winter darkness but flourishing when light returns the following spring. As the vast area of pack ice starts to break up in the summer, the algae are released into the sea, a production almost equal to that of the phytoplankton below, and greatly increasing the availability of food to other animals.

Although the harsh polar world allows the survival of only a few terrestrial organisms with extreme adaptations, the seas offer a stable, relatively moderate environment, with temperatures remaining just below freezing year-round. Because cold water holds more dissolved oxygen than when it is warm, and because summer sunlight allows continuous photosynthesis by these thriving algae, the resulting super-

Gentoo penguins tend their young on a rocky ledge above Port Lockroy as dawn catches the awesome ridges on Anvers Island. Blue-eyed shags nest freely among the gentoos in this intimate little rookery. Lockroy has a fine natural harbour that became popular during whaling days. It was then occupied during World War II by the British, who set up a small wooden hut in a secret military operation known as Tabarin. Today Port Lockroy is a common anchorage for yachts and tour vessels. (CM)

Penguins often use floating bergs as "excursion boats," refuges that afford a restful break from foraging. Here, chinstrap penguins float by on a rounded berg in the Weddell Sea, between Paulet Island and the Antarctic Sound. (RN)

abundance of food in the ocean is the key to the riches of life in the Deep South.

In the Southern Ocean the food chain is foreshortened, often consisting of only three links: microalgae–krill–penguin, or perhaps microalgae–krill–whale. These variations upon a common theme are always simple, with krill as the keystone, enabling the energy captured by the primary producers to rise efficiently to all levels of this delicately balanced ecosystem. This in turn permits a staggering profusion of relatively small numbers of species. There are only some 160 vertebrates in the Southern Ocean, about 120 of which are fish. Antarctic waters have always supported the greatest numbers of baleen whales, along with the most numerous seal in the world, the crabeater. There are estimates of over 75 million penguins and seabirds winging their way over these heaving waves.

All these species rely on the tremendous productivity of the Southern Ocean for their sustenance. The total amount of krill itself is not known, with stocks conservatively considered to be in the tens of millions of tons, but even this estimate varies as much as thirty-fold. Whatever the final figure, and most likely the total fluctuates naturally from year to year, many hundreds of thousands of tons of krill are consumed annually by the fish, squid, whales, seals, penguins, and flying birds of the Deep South. This teeming life in a teeming sea is all geared and bound to the seasonal ebb and flow of the inanimate ice. To the plants and animals of the Antarctic waters, the ice is home.

Along the broken fringes of the pack ice, open leads provide rich feeding grounds for large numbers of Adélie penguins. Between bouts of diving they often jump onto the ice floes to preen and rest. This strategy also helps them to evade leopard seals, their major predators, which frequently lurk submerged along the edges of the sea ice. (MJ)

Trying to maneuver on the ice blocks' slick surface, these Adélies near Hope Bay are carefully measuring their next steps before resigning themselves to leaping into the sea. (TDR)

The Uninvited Guest

Ice crystals in the atmosphere form a perfect halo around a pale, watery sun high over the peaks of the Gerlache Strait. (CM)

(Opposite)

This long view shows the impressive valley known as Bailey Head on Deception Island. (TDR)

In contrast to the exquisite balance that exists between the Antarctic environment and its living organisms, Antarctica is as alien to humans as humans are to it. Yet conversely the raw power and ungraspable wildness of its nature endow the frozen south with irresistible magnetism to anyone with a yen for adventure or discovery. I have been lucky enough to venture into this wondrous region on many occasions, to be amidst the wildlife that abounds there and to experience the grandeur and overwhelming beauty surrounding the normal daily routines of so many individual lives. In this prodigious realm I am forever finding new and stimulating events that, in their simplicity, not only enrich my own life but in subtle ways serve to give it renewed direction.

Sometimes such instances may be small things, almost insignificant, that could easily have gone unnoticed. One such occasion occurred as I watched the social activities of a group of gentoo penguins. Shuttling laboriously back and forth along a well-worn path in the snow, one penguin at the edge of the colony was busy stealing small stones from an irate neighbor some distance away and carrying them back to its nest. Perhaps a commonplace scene, except that each time the thief was away on another raid its own nearest neighbor simply reached over and promptly redistributed the booty by building new additions to its own nest.

There are also times when the most significant events may be a spectacular new vista, a bizarrely crevassed glacier, some fleeting play of light on the icy slopes of a steep mountain, or the fury of foam whipping from wave tops as the sudden rush of an impending katabatic wind sweeps down the frozen valleys of adjacent peaks. The blue berg, with the penguins all but oblivious to its demise, will always remain one of the most gripping spectacles I have ever witnessed. There is for me an incredibility about being in Antarctica: seeing and feeling the power of this utter wilderness, yet knowing that I could never be a part of it fills me with awe and respect. I hope Antarctica will not know when I am there or that I have ever been there, for when I walk uninvited in a world that is home to so many beings other than my own, it is the least I can do to try and be as insignificant as possible. This, for me, is the very essence of visiting the Antarctic. It is here, too, that I find myself infinitely saddened in realizing how widely at variance our role as a species often is from this simple concept of minimal impact.

Each time I return to my cabin after spending hours on deck while cruising the Southern Ocean, I cannot fail to feel a sense of emptiness in this vast rich ocean where the gigantic blue whale used to roam in great numbers. A mammal thirty meters long and weighing 180 tons, the

Loose drifting pack ice surrounds Peter I Island, causing vessels approaching the island to proceed with caution. The steep, rugged island was first sighted in 1821 by the Russian explorer Bellingshausen, who named it after Peter the Great, founder of the Russian navy. (CM)

southern blue is the largest animal the earth has ever known, larger than its northern kin and larger even than the mightiest of dinosaurs. Its slightly smaller cousin, the fin whale, used to be the most common whale in the world, and the leviathan of legends, the enormous male sperm whale, used Antarctica as its migratory destination. Prey to the harpoons of modern whaling fleets, all have dwindled to shadows of their former numbers. Some remain, especially the smaller species, although they are still being pursued to this day.

I have experienced magical moments with playful humpbacks, rare and yet so trusting, deep in the quiet fjords of Antarctica. Rolling, spy-hopping, lob-tailing, and blowing so close to my small boat as to douse its occupants, they showed nothing but gentle curiosity in the presence

The low rays of a late austral summer day twist and bend in unusual ways. The narrow Lemaire Channel, with its surrounding tall peaks, lends itself to this kind of interchange of scenery and soft light. (RN)

of a species that has spent centuries trying to spell their doom. Other days I have observed family pods of hunting orcas or the speedy maneuvers of the slender minke, still victimized by the hundreds under the thin disguise of Japanese science.

But I remember the accounts of the mariners of past centuries describing entire days when the horizon would be filled with wispy whale blows, and the still of the night would be accompanied by the resounding whoosh of the animals surfacing to breathe. I try in vain to imagine these past scenes, which I would dearly love still to exist. The majority of the great whales, however, are gone. I have never seen a southern blue, and with only one thousand or so left by my fellow humans to ply the entire Southern Ocean, the chances are remarkably slight that I ever will.

Echoes of Change

The Antarctic comprises three discrete yet totally interdependent entities: the continent, the Southern Ocean, and the atmosphere. These combine to create the whole that is Antarctica—a tenth of our world. Not surprisingly, the entire globe is affected by its existence, and indeed it is this great cold void that in a complex series of metaphysical reactions maintains the dynamics of the world's atmospheric energy balance. If it were not for this balance the tropical and subtropical regions would become hotter and more humid, while the ice cap, conversely, would become progressively colder. Our world is an intricate web of interrelated phenomena, no part of which can function independently of the rest, no part of which can be abused without harming the whole.

There are many facts that suggest we are abusing our world drastically. Carbon dioxide levels are 25 percent higher than they were one generation ago. Global temperature has increased by over half a degree since last century. A thinning of the ozone layer above Antarctica is recurring yearly. We continue to discharge gases that are known to destroy ozone in the upper atmosphere; even with the accepted knowledge that carbon dioxide does lead to climatic warming, we continue to release it in such quantities that its atmospheric volume will double during a person's life span, with a prospective temperature rise of at least 2 degrees centigrade.

Global warming is now a commonplace term, having acquired an almost homely quality in many a conversation, yet its consequences will be dire. With most major cities lying only just above sea level, the ice cap would only have to melt a fraction before many would be swamped. Humankind is adaptable, but there are many species that will not be able to support even the most subtle variations and will suffer massive die-offs. Such subtle variations are already occurring; skin cancer in humans is more prevalent than only a few years ago. But we have little information on what may be happening right now in the natural world. The most susceptible species are often the lower forms of life, those forming the foundation of the food chain and upon which all other life depends. Imperiling these primary producers will cause the results to ricochet through to the top members. The impact will have us reeling.

The reduction of the protective ozone layer, which filters out most of the sun's ultraviolet rays, is allowing intensified solar radiation to reach the earth's surface. In the last several years it has been discovered that this radiation can seriously hamper the health and growth of diatoms, the single-celled algae upon which krill feed, and possibly of the krill population itself. It is not unreasonable to assume that such a decline would trigger dramatic changes in the Antarctic ecosystem. As if this po-

(Opposite)

Brash ice contrasts with distant bergs near Torgersen Island. Even reduced to tinkling brash, the power and mystery of ice are not lost. (TDR)

tential alone were not sobering enough, the massive commercial harvesting of krill as a packaged high-protein food for humans and their livestock is already a booming business for some nations, compounding the reduced supply of this staple for the legitimate Antarctic residents. Until we learn in detail the functioning of such a vast portion of the planet and understand the changes that we are already causing in the southern seas, surely we cannot justify the current moves to exploit it.

The Endless Journey

Antarctic ice, as tangible as it is, as immutable as it may seem, is ephemeral, errant, always in a state of flux, eternally in pursuit of some unattainable stability. Although permanent as a whole, no part of the ice cap is fixed, but is rather a small step in the continuum. An ice crystal is as transient as the water molecule from which it is composed. The last melting fragment of a berg lost at the fringes of the Southern Ocean is but a vestige of its former self, a pale reminder of its past glory, yet it is also on the verge of renewal. To see its death is also to witness its rebirth back into the endless cycle of water, snow, and ice.

Water evaporates off the ocean to rise into the cold upper atmosphere, where ice crystals first form as snow around microscopic dust particles. Snow can fall wherever conditions are right—where lower air layers and surface temperatures are cold enough to prevent its melting. In Antarctica the conditions are always right. As snow settles over the continent it is blown by the winds, redistributed, drifted, and packed into ridges, ripples, and dunes as if it were desert sand. This material can be light and porous or it can be hard as granite, the identity of the delicate snowflakes lost and destroyed, transformed into solid, battered grains of ice. In a kind of glazed inland sea sculpted by the wind, this drifting can form gentle static waves, or rear up into rigid breakers like frozen surf two meters high, called sastrugi. On the interior expanses of the polar plateau, snowfall may be less than five centimeters per year. Yet inexorably, as new layers are added the young ice crystals are pressed downward into the ice cap. Under the weight of their own burden the lower layers are compressed, tempered by the intense cold and pressure, consolidated into a dense, impermeable mass of glacial ice. This load, some 30 million cubic kilometers in volume, actually depresses the underlying rock of the continent by about 900 meters, sinking much of it below sea level. Recent satellite imagery of the earth shows that our globe is in fact pear-shaped, deformed as a result of this icy dome.

As hundreds of thousands of years of snows accumulate on the polar plateau, the aging crystals descend ever deeper, incorporating into the resulting matrix a record of atmospheric particles trapped by snowfall through the ages. Like a vast information bank, this record can be read, layer by layer, by drilling deep core samples. Evidence of past climatic changes, intensive meteor rains, and major volcanic eruptions—in short, the state of the earth's atmosphere since prehistoric times—can be traced. In the uppermost strata are indications of the pollution caused by the Industrial Revolution and the first atomic bomb detonations, stark reminders of humanity's own activities etched into these natural archives.

But the ice sheet is not static. It is a dynamic system, a moving body. As the crystals are forced onward by new additions from above they will travel not only down, but also outward toward the edges of the continent. Ice flows, albeit quite slowly, under the influence of gravity. It flows as frozen streams, major courses leading away from the ice shed. And it flows as huge glaciers that collect, drain, and transport ice from the sheet along unseen corridors, gradually shunting thousands of years of ice out toward the coast. Antarctica's Lambert Glacier, outlet for about a quarter of the major ice sheet, is the world's largest—over 40 kilometers wide and flowing for 400 kilometers.

As a glacier travels, at speeds ranging from a few meters to two kilometers per year, terrific stresses are created throughout its body. At its lower levels a slower kind of plastic, almost reluctant, movement carries the bulk of the glacier over the terrain, allowing the upper layers to glide more quickly. The ice deforms, then stretches, cracks, groans, and creaks, eventually succumbing to the forces that are tearing it apart. Immense crevasses open, fissuring the surface into a tortured mosaic of deep scars. But the flow of the glacier remains steady and unrelenting, almost methodical in its advance. It will change direction to find the easiest route, snaking along hidden valleys, dividing to skirt around unyielding peaks, eddying in natural basins. Ruthlessly gouging and scouring the rock below, and carving the mountains lining its path, it carries the debris away with it as it heads for the sea.

Most glaciers end at the shores, where their steep leading edges regularly calve along stress lines, loud cracks and booms heralding the release of the ice into the ocean. Freed at last from millennia of captivity inside the dark depths of the ice cap, the ice crystals spring forth as icebergs to wander in new directions across the sea. No longer protected within the confines of the ice sheets, they will be fully exposed to the destructive nature of their new environment. After surviving hundreds

Ice is the beginning of
Antarctica and ice is its
end. As one moves from
perimeter to interior, the
proportion of ice relentlessly
increases. Ice creates more
ice, and ice defines ice.

STEPHEN PYNE
The Ice: A Journey to Antarctica

*Ice in several of its Antarctic incarnations
is juxtaposed against an aerial view of
floes in the Ross Sea. Clockwise from top
of opposite page: spikey iceberg details;
Dry Valley ice at Lake Vanda; wind-
sculpted snow at Cape Evans; iron-hard
sastrugi on the polar plateau; volcanic
ash layers on Deception Island; and
crevasse icicles near Scott Base.*

of thousands of years and having migrated several hundred kilometers since descending as snowflakes onto the polar plateau, the ice crystals will soon revert to water and thence to vapor rising back into the eternally frozen skies of Antarctica.

March of the Giants

The mightiest bergs of all are released from the great ice shelves, as are the majority of all bergs. Many glaciers and ice streams flow out into the vast flat expanses of floating ice that fill fjords and large embayments indenting the shores of Antarctica. Rising and falling daily with the tidal cycle, these shelves are grafted to the land at their roots and are constantly being flexed at a boundary line known as the hinge zone. Their seaward margins are dominated by immense vertical ice cliffs over thirty meters high and often extending 200 meters below the waterline. Fed simultaneously from numerous sources, they may be many thousands of square kilometers in area; the largest, the Ross Ice Shelf, is equivalent to the size of France.

Pushed steadfastly forward by the advancing glaciers that feed them, with infiltrating seawater slowly prying open cracks and fissures into gaping rifts and chasms, the leading edges of these shelves undergo huge break-offs. Tabular icebergs are thus born. They can be giants thousands of meters long, the largest known being about the size of Belgium, and may be tracked for many years in their wanderings as they are ferried along at the whim of the coastal currents and winds. Occasionally they collide with other shelves and ice tongues, generating new bergs in the process, or they themselves may calve, dividing into smaller entities. Sometimes they become grounded in bays or trapped in a gyre, remaining near the coast and enduring for a decade or more before finally breaking loose into the Southern Ocean. Drifting through the seasons, a large tabular berg may witness the growth and decline of the winter pack again and again, being recaptured by the sea ice each time the rolling ocean is quieted by its icy cloak.

As the autumn days of March become shorter and the air temperature drops, the sea begins to freeze, unobtrusively, almost surreptitiously. Spicules of frazil ice start to grow and float to the surface, giving the sea a greasy appearance. Hesitant at first, the delicate crystalline needles form the foundation for the imminent expansion of Antarctica's frozen limits. Soon the grease ice coagulates, consolidating into platelets that are jostled by the motion of the waves, the edges curling as they rub

(Opposite)

This small iceberg has turned completely over after being eroded by wave action. It is now grounded in the entrance to Arthur Harbor near the United States's Palmer Station. (CM)

together to produce pancake ice. This in turn fuses, becoming thicker as new ice congeals below and snow collects on the surface, eventually damping the waves and blanketing the sea in a white mantle as much as ten meters thick: the pack. At the peak of the freeze the advance of pack ice is phenomenal, extending to nearly 3,000 kilometers from the coast, its outer margin gaining 4 kilometers per day, or over 2.5 meters a minute. Yet the pack is not solid. Constantly shifting, the ice is broken up by the long ocean swells and set in motion by winds and currents. Eddies in the current can produce almost permanent clearings of open water called polynyas, or a vague shift in the wind direction may open a lead, only for it to close again in an instant. Unwary vessels have been drawn into such navigable stretches and ultimately been trapped for lengthy periods. Storms exert a tremendous force on the pack, cramming the floes together, driving them on top of each other, and causing huge pressure ridges that have the power to crush almost anything in their way, driving many an unfortunate ship into the sea below and then concealing the grave as if the intruder had never dared to exist.

Even the almighty icebergs are captured by the pack, but never for long. Driven by the same winds and currents that motivate the pack itself, but more efficiently, a berg often plows on through, oblivious to the ice grinding against its sides, steadily advancing, seemingly propelled by some inner force, striving to break free. Ultimately, as the sun returns to the south, the melting pack begins to break up and relinquish its hold on the sea. Gradually reduced to a fraction of its winter spread, 80 percent of the Antarctic pack ice remains in this perennial state of ebb and flow. And the bergs are freed once more.

One of the most enduring spectacles of maritime Antarctica is the awesome migration of tabular icebergs past the tip of the Antarctic Peninsula. They spill forth from the frozen vastness of the Weddell Sea, born from its countless ice shelves and pushed north and west by its spiraling currents. Through the narrow Antarctic Sound they jostle, angular, flat-topped, like colossal giants on the march. Ponderously they ram together, abrading each other's smooth, crystalline faces and reshaping the sides of small volcanic islands in their way. As far as the eye can see they crowd the horizon, many so enormous that, from the deck of a ship, it is impossible to determine where one begins and the other ends.

About 5,000 to 10,000 major bergs are calved yearly from Antarctica, and as they go they carry away parts of the continent. Slowly decaying and melting, they disseminate their cargo of glacial rubble, long since scoured from the land, to the far reaches of the Southern Ocean. But as they wane the bergs also unleash a new source of energy, which they

(Opposite)

A group of Adélie penguins rests and preens peacefully on a small berg while behind the intricate spires and arches of the "blue berg" command attention. Less than a minute after this photograph was taken, the blue berg started to break up, causing the sea to roll, waves almost washing the penguins from their retreat. (MJ)

Glittering white, shining blue, raven black, in the light of the sun, the land looks like a fairy tale. Pinnacle after pinnacle, peak after peak—crevassed, wild as any land on our globe, it lies, unseen and untrodden.

ROALD AMUNDSEN
after discovering the
Queen Maud Range in 1911.

A fog bank hovers at Half Moon Island. The climate changes so quickly that one feels as if exposed to a huge respirator of weather. (TDR)

Surrounded by graceful alpine peaks, Paradise Bay is one of the most spectacular spots on the entire Antarctic Peninsula. (CM)

(Opposite)

Through such sights as these reflections of late afternoon light in the Lemaire Channel, Antarctica challenges one's senses and sensibilities. (RN)

acquired eons ago when the falling snows captured nitrates from the atmosphere. Now liberated, these stores of nutrients foster life in the tight community encircling the berg, a small icy world within a world of ice. Localized plankton blooms become the focus for other animals, all present to reap the harvest sown by the ice. Entirely geared to the sea ice, the beautiful white snow petrel makes its living exclusively around bergs or amongst the pack.

Still the bergs wander on, leaving their homeland yet reverting to their origins, weathering away. At sea a berg will live through rough spells and calm, dull days and bright, on its one-way voyage. On the finer

days it will decay faster, as its surface melts and forms ice swamps in its valleys and hollows, the runoff fluting its sides. A large berg many even create its own weather, one day masking its contours under a veil of fog, or perhaps on a clear morning producing a wispy halo of cloud, a tiny microclimate within the immensity of the Southern Ocean. Many bergs may swarm together, swept by the same current, or a freak eddy may catch a solitary berg, leading it astray, then abandoning it as a lonely outcast left to meander its own path, possibly serving one last time as a resting post for penguins.

What is certain is that every berg is dying, becoming ever smaller. Far from the shelter of land or the pack, it will probably not survive more than a season or two. Sea and meltwater seep into its many cracks and fissures—either old scars from its ice field days, or new wounds opened by the beating waves. Chunks break off. Growing unstable, it may tilt or roll, revealing smooth water-worn undersides and wave-cut terraces. The weaker parts cave in. And always it melts. Occasionally a berg may even breach the bounds of Antarctica, crossing the Convergence and entering warmer waters that only serve to erode it more quickly. There is no escape.

But for some, death does not come so gradually. Perhaps under the darkening skies of an impending storm, as an aging berg lumbers over the long ocean swells, waves beating at its flanks, a vibration will build up within its tired ice. Beginning as a faint tremor, a rhythmic cadence spreads throughout its body, exciting its very molecules until all are echoing with the common theme, a natural frequency. Then abruptly, with the same efficiency with which a pure soprano voice can explode a wine glass, the berg shatters, disintegrates, and leaves in its wake a mere stream of brash ice and bits to mark its passing. The berg is no more. The cycle is complete.

Graceful snow-covered peaks in the Gerlache Strait surround the entrance to Port Lockroy harbor. During 1897–99 the Belgian Adrien de Gerlache made the first survey of the Gerlache Strait and what is now called the Danco Coast. Gerlache's Belgica *became the first vessel to be trapped in Antarctic ice and suffer an enforced overwintering.* (CM)

Solar Message

Seasons of Life around the Antarctic Peninsula

Sea, land, and sky all speak of change. The ocean, held captive in frozen stillness by months of frigid temperatures, now rises and falls with renewed vigor. In rhythmic cadence, each swell hurtles against the dark shore, carrying with it all the accrued momentum of the Southern Ocean. Upon its back ride a thousand fragments of ice like opalescent glass, churning, crashing, polishing the shingled beach. Larger bergs are grounded offshore while smaller shards lay stranded by the tide. Remnants of winter, they squeak and groan, slowly disintegrating. It is early spring at Harmony Cove.

The breeze, now gentle, is heavy with fog. Moisture drips from my hair. Everywhere the snow, soft and sagging, is melting into rivulets and pools, revealing the backbone of the land. Tortuous pinnacles of rock, encrusted with lichens, glow orange and gray in the dull light, while hilltops, already blown clear of snow, loom brilliant green with freshly exposed banks of moss and algae. This is Nelson Island, part of the South Shetland Islands bordering the western tip of the Antarctic Peninsula. This northern extension of the continent outside the polar circle, where temperatures are comparatively mild, is often called the "Banana Belt of Antarctica." It is here that much of the Antarctic wildlife is concentrated.

From where I stand, the sea looks dark and foreboding, without horizon. From a pool of gray water amongst the brash ice, a band of penguins suddenly erupts onto the shore. Chinstrap penguins. Nervously they squawk and look around as if amazed by their own boldness. Shaking the water from their plumage, they toddle up the snowy valley and disappear into the mist. Every few minutes new arrivals follow to join the huge colony already staked out high on the snow-free hillsides. It is probably the first time this season they have set foot on land, having spent six months or more at the twilight edge of the winter pack ice. At last the sun is moving south again, flooding the frozen continent with life-giving light. And with it the message is spreading to all living orga-

(Opposite)

A giant petrel casts watery reflections in the Drake Passage. The Antarctic continent is surrounded by 10 percent of the world's oceans, a mystical realm unknown to us humans. Seabirds, however, have mastered this watery habitat, and we must marvel at their skill and grace in playing the troughs and wind flows for their own maximum benefit. (TDR)

nisms of the season of plenty just ahead, and consequently of the urge to breed. The process begins at the lowest levels among the microscopic plant forms inhabiting the sea, snow, and ice, and spreads rapidly through the food chain. The arrival of light makes photosynthesis possible, and with it the growth and development of all life. As the days grow longer the penguins move south through the fragmenting sea ice, unfailingly making their way back to their natal rookeries through the great fog banks so common in this region. Where exactly they have spent the winter no one knows; they have been at the whim of the drifting pack and food supply. But now they take to the land in vast numbers, reclaiming their ancestral rookeries as soon as the ground is freed of its burden of snow and ice, with a sense of urgency born of millions of years of fine-tuned adaptation to the Antarctic's extreme environment. Within a few short weeks they must claim territories, find mates, hatch eggs, raise young, molt, and be ready to depart once again, ahead of the freezing ocean.

With the coming of spring seabirds are taking to the land in wave after living wave. Through the kelp and onto the verdant headlands of South Georgia come throngs of macaroni penguins, while into the mountains of the Antarctic continent, far to the south, Antarctic petrels are flocking. On Bouvet Island, the most distantly isolated speck of land on earth, the influx consists of pintado and snow petrels, among others, whereas deep in the Ross Sea Adélie penguins are struggling across miles of still solid sea ice to reoccupy the world's most southerly penguin rookery. Many who have wandered the open ocean or ice margin in utter solitude now crowd into huge raucous colonies, jostling for position and space, fulfilling the fundamental need to perpetuate their kind. Stress will take its toll of life, while predators and accidents claim others. Whatever the species and wherever the location, the return of the sun heralds the arrival of all those following its seasonal path of productivity.

The trusting humpback whale, reduced to a fraction of its former population, still follows a yearly migration spanning thousands of miles between more tropical calving grounds and rich coastal feeding areas along the shores of Antarctica. After spending most of the day feeding near the surface, this whale began enthusiastically lob-tailing, or slapping the water with its fluke, perhaps as a signal to its companion nearby. Although humpbacks are now officially protected worldwide, some whaling still continues in Antarctic waters. (TDR)

The Meeting Place

South of Nelson Island in the South Shetlands lies the active volcano of Deception Island. On its outer coast is an old weathered cinder cone called Bailey Head, whose high seaward cliffs have been deeply scoured by the relentless action of sea and ice. Great reddish-brown and ocher scars gouge its face where towering icebergs and fierce winter storms have slashed the soft volcanic substrate, leaving undercut stacks and escarpments jutting naked into the sky. In their lee is a steep, black scoria beach hemmed by a jagged, ash-tainted glacier nearly as dark as the sand.

This grandiose setting is the site of another enormous colony of chinstrap penguins. I sat there on a warm December day watching as tens of thousands of the little black-and-white birds, elegant facial markings flashing in the sunlight, went about their pressing life. All seemingly identical, everyone rushing in apparent disarray, it would have been easy to perceive only mass confusion and aimlessness, much as a visitor from space—or for that matter from another country—might see only chaos in a large airport terminal. Yet I knew that each penguin in front of me, its identity blurred perhaps by anonymity or my human lack of compre-

Humpback whales are still relatively common in the Antarctic, and it is a great joy to watch them breaching, sounding, or feeding in the clear waters of the Southern Ocean. Without disturbance you can approach them quite closely in an inflatable boat. They know exactly where you are and can time the movements of their massive bodies with great precision. (CM)

This sunset near Low Island in the upper beaches of the Antarctic Peninsula was particularly well orchestrated: fillips of wispy, red-tinged clouds above, three curious humpback whales below, nudging the Explorer *southward.* (RN)

hension, confronted a myriad of problems and responsibilities lending critical purpose to its life. In an environment where there is little room for error, no aimless penguin would live long, much less pass on its genes to future generations.

The entire inner walls of this extinct crater were speckled with nesting birds. Like a living blanket they spread as far as the eye could see, along the valleys and up the slopes of this grandest of natural amphitheaters. Already much of the snow had disappeared, leaving a quiltwork pattern of plant life and minerals. The tender green algae-clad slopes, the soft gray creek beds of volcanic ash, the black etchings of snowmelt rivulets, the sky-blue reflections of deeper streams, the lichen-covered crags, and the pinkish-white guano-painted hills where penguins crowded all created a surreal scene of interweaving color and texture unlike any other in Antarctica. The clamor of tens of thousands of voices, drifting and echoing without direction, rose and fell with the faint breeze. Even the pungent odors, probably too strong for the uninitiated, seemed gentle and appropriate, a bitter-sweet, seafood-tainted aroma that to me said only "penguin."

Sitting quite still, I was the only human present, but I was far from alone. The ship that had brought me had sailed on, and for the first time in my many visits to Antarctica I felt truly at home. The outside world had ceased to exist, or if it existed it was certainly irrelevant. As I let time

Adélie penguins may forage for eighteen to twenty-four hours or more, and up to fifty kilometers away from their nest site, before returning with a bellyful of half-digested krill. Each Adélie will do a little preening and rearranging of feathers before heading precisely to its own nest and hungry chicks. (RN)

impress the scene upon my mind, order and direction began to emerge out of this excited melee of chinstrap penguins. Forming long sinuous strings, one by one, individual penguins were leaving the colony for daily trips out to feed. Wings held out for balance, shoulders hunched and heads jutting forward, intent on keeping their footing, they walked past me uninterested on their long trek to the sea, carefully negotiating boulder fields and steep, slippery slopes. I could see their black backs toddling far down in the valley below. From the distant beach a mile or so away, new arrivals were forming similar lines up the same paths, white fronts flashing, fording rivers as they came. The motion was continuous, yet as they approached individuals would break rank and veer off into the masses on the hillside to head, with the certainty of well-hewed practice, for the one nest and mate to which each particular bird was dedicated. Indeed, here and there I witnessed moments of dramatic personal significance in their private lives. There were instances of emotional reunions or intense struggle, quiet family scenes and cases of sheer perplexity.

To my right, sidestepping through a barrage of insults from its neighbors, a returning bird stumbled up to its nest. Gaunt and guano-splattered, its sitting mate responded to the familiar call with great excitement. Ecstatic greetings followed as the two stood breast to breast, heads back, beaks wide, lost in passionate braying. In a few moments the sparkling clean bird, still dripping wet, had taken its place on the nest, while the visibly relieved mate trundled away to the sea.

Soon my attention was drawn to a different saga nearby. Where peace reigned only minutes ago, now a fierce battle erupted. Enraged beyond measure, seemingly by some utterly despicable act, the aggressor lunged forth with unrestrained fury, grabbing the culprit by the back of the head and racking it with showers of vicious blows from its bony flippers. Bewildered, the victim fled blindly, tripping over nests and slamming into brooding parents, the adversary's beak still latched onto its neck. Dust and feathers flew. Outrage spread through the squawking neighborhood. Together the quarreling birds tumbled down a scree embankment before the matter was finally settled. They stood up at last, shook themselves and walked off. One moved down the valley, looking nervous and unsettled, while the other, indignant, returned to its nest. Of the thousands of other penguins present at this moment not one seemed to matter to either of the two. What deep personal feuds, what dastardly deeds to avenge, I wondered, could possibly fuel such seething anger in a bird's small mind?

Because penguins return to their breeding colonies at the beginning of spring when the land is still covered with its shroud of snow, they tend to aggregate around the higher or more exposed regions. Although the birds often have to walk long distances—up to a mile is quite common—these areas are more quickly freed of snow as the summer advances and are less likely to become too muddy or flooded with meltwater. (MJ)

An Adélie fixes its piercing gaze. This particular bird has raised its head feathering, indicating annoyance. These brush-tailed penguins stand their ground at the approach of intruders. (MJ)

Adélie penguins swim offshore of Torgersen Island. (RN)

An Adélie chick's first swim may not be very pleasant. It is chilled for the first time, its genes may have alerted it to the possibility of leopards offshore, and there is no assurance that it will be able to find food as efficiently as its parents. (RN)

Later, walking slowly up a long steep corridor used as an access by most of the upper colonies, I found a lost penguin egg wedged between two small stones in the middle of the path. It was large, well-formed, and still quite fresh. Had it rolled down from one of the nests above? Had it been laid prematurely by a returning female? Soon I discovered I was not the only one to stop and ponder this egg. Straggling groups of penguins, panting in the hot morning sun, were trudging up the slope. As they reached the egg each would stop, staring at it questioningly. They cocked their heads from side to side, puzzled. Some would carefully try to roll it out of its trapped position with their beaks, much as they would turn their own eggs in their nests. After a while they moved on, only for those behind to repeat the performance.

An Adélie chick sports a "mohawk" appearance because of the last vestige of down on its head. Soon it will head to sea. After this first molt, Adélie chicks resemble their parents but lack the characteristic white eye ring. No more than 10 to 15 percent of chicks may survive to breeding age at three years, due to the Antarctic's severe weather, often scarce food, and predators like leopard seals. (RN)

An Adélie gapes at its large chick on the shoreline at Paulet Island in the Weddell Sea. The parent had just returned from a feeding run offshore, and was chased down the beach by the hungry chick. (RN)

On the high bluffs, only days short of the longest midsummer day, the activity in the colony seemed to have reached a peak. Everywhere chicks were starting to hatch, tiny wobbly heads with only half-open eyes, already stretching up with faint shrill peeps to beg for their first of numerous krill meals. Their downy coats, thin at this tender age, were almost velvety, of a pearl-gray color. Already their stomachs seemed distended, their bodies like little upturned funnels responding to their urgent need to process food as quickly as possible. Stubby feet braced against the pebble nest floor for balance, they snuggled close to their parents' warmth, minute wings still insignificant and undeveloped. In the coming weeks they would undergo dramatic changes, acquiring a thick downy insulation before reaching the full size and plumage of their parents.

Parenting is the most demanding time in the life of adult penguins. While tropical seabirds may take many months to raise their families, the Antarctic penguins have only the brief austral summer to complete their cycle. From the moment of hatching, the chicks' appetites are utterly insatiable, while their parents' ability to provide is stretched to the limit, even with the bountiful Antarctic Ocean close by.

Adélies leap onto an iceberg near Paulet Island, Weddell Sea. (RN)

Only three species of penguins make the Antarctic Peninsula and the adjacent islands their home. All three are closely related and belong to the brush-tailed penguins, *Pygoscelis*. All three are medium-sized, feed substantially on krill, and share a number of traits such as the long, rigid tail feathers that give them their name. Yet it is almost by chance that in this region they live together, sometimes nesting virtually side by side. Only the small chinstrap penguin situates the heart of its habitat around the peninsula, whereas the larger gentoo ranges around the peripheries of Antarctica. Gentoos are found mostly on oceanic islands near the Convergence and reach the continent only near its northern tip. On the other hand, for the Adélie penguin the peninsula region represents the northernmost extension of its normal breeding environment.

Stout and well-protected against the cold, the rugged little Adélies nest farther south than any other living bird, farther even than the Antarctic petrel and the majestic emperor penguin. A hardy rookery occupies Cape Royds on Ross Island, nearly 1,500 kilometers beyond the Antarctic Circle and not far from the edge of the permanent Ross Ice Shelf. Here they must brave vicious summer blizzards and sometimes kilometers of solid sea ice to commute to open water. Yet no other bird has developed a better ability to exploit the thriving undersea environment that comes to life with the summer breakup in these extreme latitudes.

Plump and stocky, marked boldly in black and white with none of the frills and adornments of its temperate cousins, the Adélie's only decorative character is its uncannily white eye rings. It is a bird that has fine-tuned the balance between the rigors of the climate and the staggering food resources by leading what seems like an accelerated life, at least during the summer. Because of its relatively small size, standing barely seventy centimeters at full stretch, it requires a high metabolism to fend off the cold. Yet it is also able to reproduce and develop at a rate so speedy as to complete its entire breeding cycle during the short summer thaw.

At the first hint of spring, while other species still linger on their winter grounds, the Adélies turn south, navigating by the returning sun toward the distant shores of the continent and its nearby islands. When open water is blocked by fast ice they continue by walking or sliding across the snow on their stomachs, heading unerringly back to the locations where they nested in previous years, and where they themselves were raised. Adequate exposed terrain is a rare commodity in this icy landscape, and not one to be given up easily. They arrive fat and healthy from their winter feeding. Males are first, and because time is so precious

Imperial (blue-eyed) shag dives under-water near Paulet Island. Shags are ungainly-looking birds but effective fishers. (TDR)

(Opposite)

The unforgettable impact of an adult chinstrap penguin's countenance is magnified by the bird's penetrating yellow eye. (RN)

here they often do not wait for their former mates, but rather pair up with any arriving female. Pebble nests are cleaned and rearranged, heated battles are fought against contending young males seeking prime space in the colony, and exuberant courtship flourishes, all in an atmosphere of feverish urgency. Soon eggs are laid, two to each nest, and the females again depart across the ice, leaving their mates to the first couple of weeks of incubation. By the time they return, the males are shadows of their former selves, having lost half of their body weight from the month or more of fasting since they left the sea.

By now summer is on its way. The bitter cold of early spring has receded, sea ice is fast dispersing, and with food supplies becoming ever more accessible an exchange of duties between mates at the nest is possible every few days. When the sooty chicks hatch after an incubation of over one month, they are tiny and vulnerable, needing protection not only against the elements but also from marauding predators such as skuas. Between nest guarding, the parents must not only feed themselves but see to the constant demands of their ever-hungry young. In a good year, responding to vast plankton blooms, krill will swarm in huge concentrations, of which the parents bring home bulging cropfuls daily. As the last snows clear, the ground turns pink and sodden from the krill-tainted guano, and the chicks grow at a phenomenal rate. Soon they are large enough to be left alone in great mobile huddles termed crèches, where their numbers protect them against both cold and predation. Swimming and porpoising at speeds of ten to fifteen kilometers per hour, parents range daily at least fifty kilometers out to sea to feed, diving repeatedly to forty or fifty meters. When they return they walk through the colony calling loudly, recognizing, among thousands of others, the eager squeaks of their own chicks who come tumbling out of the masses anxiously begging for yet another meal.

In only seven weeks Adélie chicks evolve from tiny fluff balls weighing only seventy grams to pudgy 3.5-kilo fledglings. By this time their down is replaced with new plumage, almost identical to that of their parents. Then, with the genetic exigency bred into them by countless generations of natural selection, they take to the sea, not to return for several years. Almost overnight this exodus will drain the colonies of most of their life, leaving only the haggard, feather-worn adults to linger a short while longer before they too head back to the rich shifting boundary between open ocean and pack ice that is their true home.

They are extraordinarily like children, these little people of the Antarctic world, either like children, or like old men, full of their own importance and late for dinner, in their black tail-coats and white shirt-fronts—and rather portly withal.

APSLEY CHERRY-GARRARD
The Worst Journey in the World

This jaunty chinstrap, returning to its nest site at the upper reaches of the Bailey Head colony on Deception Island, exudes confidence and enthusiasm. Indeed, the chinstraps nesting at the higher, windswept slopes of this 100,000-strong colony are the most experienced of the colony's breeders. Males rush back early in the austral spring to reclaim their precious nests and to await the return— hopefully, within days—of their mate from the previous season. (RN)

A down-covered chinstrap penguin chick stretches its wings while waiting for the other parent to return with krill. This small rookery at Waterboat Point in Paradise Bay has to put up with the debris and abandoned buildings from the Chilean station Gonzalez Videla. (CM)

In the Antarctic spring, penguins make a furious rush to return home. Early arrivals like this chinstrap on Nelson Island are often beset by freak spring storms. The snow may immobilize them and, if they've laid, render their eggs cold and lifeless. (RN)

The massive chinstrap penguin rookery at
Bailey Head on the outer rim of
Deception Island is always a hive of
activity during the summer months.
Penguins crash through the surf onto
black volcanic beaches, then climb over
loose scoria slopes to their nesting site. (CM)

Chinstrap penguins enjoy their plump, down-covered chicks on a nest of loose stones at Waterboat Point in spectacular Paradise Bay. Storm clouds gather overhead while large chunks of ice continually break off the glacier behind the bay. Two men from Cope's 1921 British Imperial Expedition spent an unplanned winter at this place, living in a crude hut fashioned from their upturned rowing boat and packing cases. (CM)

For the other two penguin species of the Antarctic Peninsula the pressures of time and climate are not nearly so acute. The little chinstrap, geared to the longer summer of these latitudes, can afford to start its nesting cycle a full month later than the Adélies nesting in the same place. Likewise the substantially larger, more northerly gentoo can wait until almost midsummer to hatch its eggs. But it is in its methods of feeding that the apparently easygoing gentoo differs most from its smaller cousins. It is not a fast swimmer, nor does it travel far out to sea, often ranging no more than twenty kilometers or so on feeding trips. Even though its staple diet is krill and fish, it takes the gentoo almost half as long to obtain the larger volumes of food as it does the others. Recent radio telemetry studies have proven that the gentoo's trick is an ability to dive far deeper than its congeners, easily exceeding 100 meters and regularly staying submerged for two minutes. Yet how it succeeds in capturing its prey in such gloomy depths remains a mystery.

The sedentary nature of the gentoo penguin is reflected throughout its life. Where the other brush-tailed penguins spend most of their year wandering the outer margins of the frozen seas, many gentoos take advantage of small areas of open water and use their capacity to dive deep below the pack to remain near land through the winter. To breed, instead of concentrating in enormous landmark rookeries they form loose colonies on sheltered headlands near their feeding grounds. The location is

Summer Serenity

A gentoo penguin enters the water at Point Lockroy. Penguins may not fly in air, but they are master fliers through water. (RN)

Gentoo penguins are catholic in both taste (fish, krill, and other marine organisms) and housing (cliffs, tussock, or flat ground, depending on the circumstance). The Antarctic Peninsula is the southern limit of gentoo distribution, the subantarctic fringe its northern limit. This Gold Harbor, South Georgia, gentoo nests in tussock, surrounded by wallowing elephant seals. (RN)

A gentoo penguin coats its bill with oil from its uropygial gland, located just above the tail. Penguins are well insulated from the incredibly cold environment: their tightly packed feathers (over seventy per square inch) are thoroughly waterproofed with this preening oil, and a blubber layer of fat provides additional protection. Their biggest problem is overheating, because excess heat can only be dissipated through barren or sparsely feathered areas at the base of the bill, on the feet, and under their wings. (TDR)

Gentoo chicks are the most attractive of the brush-tailed chicks, gleaming white below, pearly gray above. The Antarctic Peninsula represents the southern extent of their range, and they are commonly found to the north at South Georgia and the Falklands. (TDR)

A gentoo penguin brays to the sky, emitting its characteristic donkeylike belches. (MJ)

A krill-slurry dinner is about to be served for these eager gentoo chicks. Gentoos often raise both their offspring to fledging in seasons when the food supply is plentiful; otherwise, it is the stronger, most demanding sibling that receives the first serving. Hungry chicks will beg food from any adult willing to give it to them, but the parents identify their own young by their peeping sounds and beat down heavily on any rascal that tries to intrude on the feast. (MJ)

The inhabitants of a small gentoo penguin rookery on Petermann Island have a grandstand view of the southern entrance to the Lemaire Channel. (CM)

not so important to them, and they easily switch from site to site within the colony. Far more crucial is establishing a strong, stable pair bond, through which experience grows over the years. Mates frequently remain faithful through life.

The peaceful quality of a gentoo rookery comes in sharp contrast to the bustling, electric atmosphere surrounding chinstraps and Adélies. I particularly remember one late evening at Port Lockroy on Weinke Island. Low scuttling clouds danced past the sawtooth mountains on all sides. Shafts of fading gold and crimson sunlight played among the wispy curtains of mist, their filtered reflection bathing the ground in purple tones. A chill, damp wind was blowing across the water. Perfect penguin weather. Among the ancient granite boulders dozens of nesting birds sat contented. Carefully spaced, each nest was meticulously lined with a great mound of even-sized pebbles. Adults brayed gently, their orange beaks shining. Large, fat chicks, neither too hot nor too cold in their thick gray down, cuddled together sound asleep. In twos and threes, parents were traveling the age-old paths, lined with well-fertilized cushions of moss, up and down the hill. At the shore others were negotiating a thick band of wind-blown brash ice obstructing access to the sea. Bobbing and slipping, they stumbled across the heaving, jumbled carpet before disappearing into the black water. For a moment the skies opened and fiery hues enveloped the lofty peaks of neighboring Anvers Island. Then the sun sank into the twilight of an austral summer night, leaving a scene etched in stark, monochrome splendor.

At midnight on Petermann Island at the southern end of Lemaire Channel of the Antarctic Peninsula, gentoo penguins are diving in search of food for their young. The midnight sun lights up Mount Scott on the far side of Lemaire. Jean Charcot's second French expedition in 1909 wintered on Petermann Island with his vessel Pourquoi Pas? (CM)

The Meat Eaters

Just as swarming masses of krill attract vast flocks of feeding seabirds, so the numerous penguin rookeries, even though transient, draw their share of opportunistic predators. By far the most prevalent are the skuas, large rapacious relatives of the gulls. Although they are pelagic wanderers ranging far into the northern hemisphere during winter, skuas become residents when nesting, often attaching themselves to the periphery of penguin rookeries, where they glean a copious living from stolen eggs and chicks. They are intelligent and efficient, mates often cooperating to distract defensive penguin parents, only to snatch the hapless young from behind their backs. They also use teamwork to dismember their prey, leaving little to waste. In a land where there are no terrestrial birds of prey, skuas have become the top avian predators.

Similarly, in the absence of traditional carrion eaters, the giant petrels have become the leading scavengers of the southern seas. They soar on the stiff wind like the great albatrosses, and are quick to descend on anything dead or dying, from tiny storm petrel to great whale. Barely able to walk, they are not adept on land, but scour the shoreline for any morsel and are not averse to attacking any sick or unwary penguin with their formidable, self-sharpening, razor-edged beaks. When food is available intense competition easily develops, giving rise to a stringent hierarchy within their ranks.

When a freshly dead Weddell seal washed up on a beach at Nelson Island, I watched two dozen of these large birds vying for a share of the banquet. Some were dark, almost sooty in color, while others were

Skuas do much pruning around and through penguin colonies. Here, a brown skua consumes a dead Adélie, ignoring an irate living penguin nearby. Skuas have a bad reputation, but it is undeserved; they clean the colonies of the unfit. (TDR)

A pair of watchful kelp gulls surveys the sheltered waters and rugged landscape surrounding this rocky beach on Nelson Island. Areas like this are used as access ways by thousands of penguins nesting around the bases of outcroppings, as well as providing good hauling-out places for seals. (MJ)

nearly snow-white, typical of the more southerly individuals. All were intent on establishing a dominant status within the group. Hissing and cackling, they threatened and confronted each other, wings spread and tails cocked. Unwilling to back down, some would lock beaks and grapple viciously. Finally the most aggressive began staggering up the beach, while the subordinates paddled anxiously in circles nearby. Using the dead seal's eyes as the easiest entry points, within minutes they were probing up to their necks into the carcass, tearing and gobbling great bloody beakfuls of tendons and meat. More fights broke out, enabling lower-ranking petrels to get in on the feast. It was clear that within hours there would be little left of the 400-kilo seal.

Doves of Peace or Garbage Collectors?

A snowy sheathbill bathes on Half Moon Island. Sheathbills are common scavengers in the Antarctic Peninsula, and the only Antarctic bird without webbed feet. They undertake an annual migration across the Drake Passage (600 miles) to escape the rigors of the Antarctic winter. This is remarkable considering this species' inability to glide for long distances, requiring it to flap often to stay airborne. They will frequently alight on passing ships for a rest. (TDR)

(Opposite)

Pintado petrels flock on the water near Point Lookout, Elephant Island. (TDR)

If skuas are the hawks of the Antarctic and giant petrels the southern equivalent of the vultures, it is not at all clear who the snowy sheathbill is trying to impersonate. Indeed the sheathbill compares to nothing and to no one. In a land where all vertebrates pertain to the sea and all birds have webbed feet, the sheathbill struts about on chickenlike toes. It has an aversion to water and would not dream of making an honest living at sea. It occupies a niche all its own, and it almost seems to know it. Reminiscent of a dove, it appears to be distantly related to plovers. Unabashed, it lives happily off the backs of the other denizens of Antarctica. Whether the food source is a long-dead penguin, fresh seal excrement, rotten eggs, or the hapless dying victim of a leopard seal attack, all is welcome to the undiscriminating sheathbill. These birds show little objection to caking their otherwise gleaming plumage with blood and gore. In the midst of penguin rookeries they dash about with reckless disregard for irately snapping bills as they search for spilt krill or dead chicks. Not surprisingly, the penguins show unmitigated hatred for the foul little scroungers.

When adult penguins are feeding their chicks the sheathbill's cunning is fully revealed. On Elephant Island I watched one casually perched on a rock, keeping a close yet seemingly distracted eye on the feeding procedures one meter away. Again and again, the instant krill began to flow from the parent's gullet the sheathbill would swoop in from its strategic vantage point, pushing the chick's head aside with its feet to intercept the food.

In the same location I also inspected several sheathbill nests tucked prudently under large boulders. The scene I found was almost beyond belief. Squatting happily in the midst of the most indescribable filth, the dung-colored chicks sat surrounded by heaps of decaying fragments of penguins and other seabirds: heads, flippers and feet, slabs of greasy skin, bones and clumps of bloody feathers. Two chicks were busy eating a heap of unidentifiable entrails with great gusto, the rubbery, guano-covered tripe occasionally wrapping around their scraggly necks.

Only once, on the warmest day of the season, have I ever seen sheathbills get wet. On this balmy afternoon, one by one they took turns bathing heartily in a sun-warmed puddle of dubious color, in what would seem to have been their yearly bath.

Still, there is something utterly endearing about the cocky sheathbill. One of the smallest birds in Antarctica, it may hold the beggar's lot, yet it possesses the self-assurance and know-how to thrive where no other land birds exist.

Every Snow Petrel [is] a little chip off the frozen
environment that moulded it. . . . So the overall effect
of the black intrusion is that of a minute granite
nunatak peeping modestly out of a pristine snowfield.

KEITH SHACKLETON
Wildlife and Wilderness: An Artist's World

The most redoubtable of the penguins' enemies is surely the leopard seal. A large, lithe, opportunistic predator, in summer it often stalks the shallows near penguin rookeries and becomes a grisly killer. Submerged silently beneath icebergs, it will ambush home-coming penguins near shore, or lunge onto slabs of ice where they are resting. Many an Antarctic beach is littered with discarded penguin skins neatly stripped by the great carnivores, who turn them inside out with a mere shake of their jaws.

The sea leopard's massive jaw and hooked canines are also put to use on its own smaller cousin, the crabeater seal. Deep parallel scars gouging the golden coat of many a crabeater, perfectly matched to the size and shape of the leopard's maul, attest to life-and-death struggles that must often be replayed in Antarctic waters, yet have never been observed by humans. Both seals are creatures of the pack ice, spending most of their life far from our prying eyes. Indeed, almost nothing is known of the life history of leopard seals. No human has ever seen a leopard seal mate or give birth in the wild, although mothers and pups are occasionally found on the ice. From its stomach we know of many of its predatious habits and its surprisingly high reliance on krill which, like the crabeater, it may filter through sievelike teeth.

Even more mysterious is the Ross seal, denizen of the very heavy pack ice, where even today's powerful icebreakers are unable to venture. It appears not to be exceedingly rare yet our ignorance of even its most basic functions such as locomotion is staggering. The crabeater was also long thought to be a rare species, yet the advent of aerial surveys suggests it exists in prodigious numbers, perhaps up to 30 million strong, living far from land where krill is always plentiful.

Only the large Weddell seal of the coastal regions is better understood. Living farther south than any other seal, it dives deep beneath the fast ice in search of bottom-dwelling fish living in depths of up to 900 meters and, if necessary, can remain submerged for over an hour. Through the winter it gnaws at small breathing holes in the ice, rarely leaving the water. Only in the spring do females haul out around natural ice cracks to give birth, while breeding males guard the aquatic approaches below. The newborn pups are huge, already weighing twenty-five kilos, and they double that over the first ten days of life thanks to a diet of milk that is almost pure butter. By the time they are six or seven weeks old they have more than quadrupled their birth weight, and their mothers leave them to begin life on their own.

This arrangement is quite different from that of the elephant and fur seals of the northern peripheries of Antarctica where, without the con-

A leopard seal yawns near Hope Bay. The fearsome leopard is the penguins' main predator in the water, but on land leopards are quite harmless. (TDR)

(Opposite)

A snow petrel shows its days-old chick in a nest crevice on Coronation Island, South Orkneys. (RN)

139

Fur seals have rebounded in large numbers in the Scotia Arc and northern Antarctic Peninsula. They are dangerous creatures, especially when the old "wigs" have collected their harems during the breeding season early in the Antarctic spring. (TDR)

Beauty and grace are performed whether or not we will or sense them. The least we can do is try to be there.

ANNIE DILLARD
Pilgrim at Tinker Creek

(Opposite)

A bull elephant seal may have as many as fifteen females in his harem. They seem to take great pleasure in lying in a tangled huddle in the foulest places imaginable near the beach. Sometimes pups get crushed in the melee. (CM)

This crabeater seal has hitched a ride on a small ice floe and is drifting past the Adélie penguin rookery on Torgersen Island. It is close to this location that the Argentinian vessel Bahia Paraiso struck a reef in January 1989, disgorging a significant amount of fuel. (CM)

A crabeater seal scratches its open mouth. These are the world's most numerous seals, perhaps over 30 million. Their name, however, is a misnomer, since they feed almost exclusively on krill. (TDR)

Weddell seals can dive to depths of at least 900 meters in search of food such as Mawsonii "cod." Year-round, they must maintain a breathing hole in the sea ice. Much of the summer is spent sleeping around the edge of their holes, the females nursing their pups with thick creamy milk. (CM)

A leopard seal shows its snakelike head at Martel Inlet. Leopards are fascinating creatures, taking many penguins as sustenance but also quite adept at fishing if necessary. (RN)

143

A Weddell seal sprawls on black sand. While ashore, Weddells have the appearance of overgrown puppies contrary to their aquatic prowess. They can dive to at least 900 meters and are able to survive the brutal Antarctic winter by chewing breathing holes through the ice. (RN)

venient commodity of ice floes, the animals must gather from their ocean wanderings into huge breeding assemblages. It is these assemblages that made them vulnerable to the savage onslaughts of the oil and fur hunters of centuries past, who slaughtered them by the hundreds of thousands almost to the last individuals.

In view of our blundering mistakes of the past, it seems bizarre at the very least that some still write of the Antarctic seals as "a vast natural resource that has been virtually completely untapped." I had taken little notice of such words when Antarctica had seemed to live only in my imagination, and I had avidly read any available scientific literature. But when I stood on an Antarctic shore, with a dozen Weddell seals peacefully asleep on a carpet of red seaweed, with wind and wave and the crash of distant calving glaciers the only sounds, the full significance of a potential sealing industry suddenly stood out like crimson blood on the snowbanks. As a small cluster of curious penguins trustingly inspected the tip of my boot, I felt a flash of hope that perhaps after all humankind would someday come to treat the world's wild living beings with the respect and, yes, aesthetic consideration they deserve, rather than with cold detachment. I vowed that if Antarctica were to live, its beauty and magic, its endless ability to set the spirit free, must be shared—through words, pictures, or preferably direct personal adventure—with all who yearn to feel such peace.

The largest predator of all in Antarctica is a mammal. The elegant orca ranges as far south as there are open waters for it to swim, preying heavily on both penguins and seals. The large size of many whale species makes them ideal candidates for life in cold seas. Coupled with supreme blubber insulation and efficient heat-retaining circulation, their bulk makes them all but oblivious to low water temperatures.

Resisting heat loss is the number one prerequisite for all life in Antarctica, and indeed in most warm-blooded species evolutionary themes to this end recur often. Penguins, seals, and whales all possess a thick layer of subcutaneous fat, and all have extremely reduced appendages. Size is essential, since volume increases much faster than body surface, again favoring heat retention. Yet for some this adaptation also presents serious obstacles; most penguins, for example, must be able to grow to their full size within quite a short time. While mammals have the advantage of milk production to boost the growth of their young, penguins can afford to remain much smaller while sharing the same frigid waters by adding the extra protection of an amazingly efficient covering of feathers. Indeed, a penguin's plumage is denser than that of any other bird, with over eleven feathers per square centimeter, overlapping like scales and trapping a layer of air within a thick lining of underfluff. Preened and oiled to maintain complete waterproofing, the penguin's plumage keeps the bird warm and dry even after months at sea, and must be changed only once a year. Without this protection it would be quite impossible for an organism of similar size to survive submerged in an ocean that is near freezing year-round.

Birds in general are adept in cold climates. Not only are they doubly insulated with feathers and fat, but they also possess a high metabolism enabling them to process calories rapidly, and a mobility allowing them to follow the most suitable seasonal conditions with ease. It is therefore not surprising that there are many more varieties of birds in Antarctica than of any other air-breathing life forms. While penguins may be the most celebrated in terms of their exquisite adaptations, tube-nosed seabirds also have a substantial presence. Compared to five species of Antarctic penguins, no less than twenty-four tube-nosed seabirds ride the turbulent air currents of the Southern Ocean. They range from the regal albatrosses to the tiniest storm petrels and prions. All travel the high seas as free as the wind, many using the very energy of the waves to glide over the heaving air cushions without a flap of their wings and coming to land only reluctantly to breed. Some, such as the miniature Wilson's storm petrel, range far and wide across the globe in winter—almost into the Arctic—while others, such as the Antarctic and snow petrels, never stray far from the southern ice. For the wandering albatross the great Southern Ocean is an endless pathway to the east, circling unimpeded around the world near the Convergence, where no landmass obstructs its passage. Many of the smaller petrels are krill and plankton feeders, whereas some, like the beautiful pintados, do not hesitate to take advantage of any scavenging opportunities, descending in noisy flocks onto the drifting carcasses of dead whales or seals.

Only a handful of other seabirds make Antarctica their home. In some ways resembling the penguins, the blue-eyed or imperial cormorant is a coastal diver that pursues small fish in the rocky shallows. The elegant Antarctic tern also remains close to shore, where it plunge dives for small fish and krill, only rarely meeting its migrating northern relative, the Arctic tern. Perhaps the most surprising of the southern seabirds is the scavenging kelp gull, resembling the black-backed gull of the north; its breeding range around South America, Australia, and South Africa seems to reach Antarctica almost as an afterthought.

Our understanding of the dynamics of all these Southern Ocean birds, like that of the seals, remains scanty at best. Efforts have repeatedly been made to assess their biomass, the sum total of their living weight. In order to justify the human exploitation of krill, even greater emphasis is placed on quantifying their total food consumption, perhaps reaching 100 million tons of krill per year. Yet no one has been able to study the diet and feeding habits of oceanic birds in winter other than circumstantially, lending, as always, a frightening quality to any assertions of "rational exploitation" in the far south.

Winds of Autumn

The new year is still young on the Antarctic Peninsula when the subtle portents of winter begin to appear. The nights grow colder and darker than they are at Christmastime. On quiet mornings it is not rare to see the symmetrical patterns of grease ice on the surface of calm bays, the first tentative ice crystals forming over the sea. Everywhere large gentoo chicks begin to explore their new world, wandering to the shoreline, wading into meltwater ponds and streams, and generally investigating all that seems intriguing to their young minds.

The fall exodus begins almost surreptitiously. I had been traveling about the peninsula for some weeks, calling at one of the large Adélie rookeries on King George Island regularly. I had seen the sooty chicks

A constant flow of Adélie penguins, their passage staining the snow connecting the huge Hope Bay rookery with the sea, moves up and down the ice ramp, shuttling cropfuls of food back to their growing chicks inland. (TDR)

fatten almost by the day, becoming ever more agile and adventurous as they began to change into their black-and-white subadult plumage. But I was still unprepared when I returned one last time in February to find the hillsides suddenly bare. Pink, guano-stained mud was puddling in the rain amongst the rocks. The wind whistled as mist swirled around bright, lichen-splattered pinnacles of columnar basalt. Mummified penguin carcasses, attesting to those disfavored by chance or by genes, lay embedded in the trodden ground, a testimony of life that was. Not a sound, not a movement remained of the bustling penguin metropolis that had been on the island only days earlier, its members now porpoising unseen out to sea ahead of the ice. Only those life forms unable to

The Antarctic Peninsula, sometimes called the "banana belt" of the continent, is emblazoned with colorful, lichen-laden rocks. (CM)

A man doesn't begin to attain wisdom until he recognizes that he is no longer indispensable.

RICHARD BYRD
Alone

depart were beginning to wind down into the deep dormancy that would see them through the winter.

If life in the Antarctic seas thrives in impressive multitudes, the scene on the continent is a striking contrast by any standards. Not a single species of vertebrate can survive here, leaving a few insects, mites, and nematodes as the sole representatives of the entire animal kingdom. Even plants are not considerably ahead. A small grass, *Deschampsia antarctica,* and an even smaller pearlwort, *Colobanthus quitensis,* are the only two vascular plants in existence. The lower orders of mosses and algae fare somewhat better. Only lichens, those strange organisms consisting of the combined efforts of both fungi and algae and capable of suspending all their life functions for months on end, successfully cling to some of the most inhospitable locations. The low temperatures maintained by the huge volume of the Antarctic ice cap, even in summer, and the desiccating effect of the wind combine to make Antarctica far more hostile to life than similar latitudes in the Arctic.

Another factor is the shear scarcity of available land. An overwhelming 99 percent of the entire continent of Antarctica is permanently covered in snow and ice. And much of the remaining 1 percent is found on wind-scoured vertical faces where life has only the remotest chance of establishing itself. It is not surprising, then, that nesting seabirds on the continent must crowd into tightly packed spaces along the shorelines.

It is along the shoreline regions that humans, for numerous reasons, have increasingly imposed their presence. The first time I sailed into Paradise Bay, deep among the breathtaking mountains of the Antarctic Peninsula, I was as elated as any before me. Row upon row of immaculate peaks rose into the crystalline sky. Fluted turquoise and blue icebergs of all shapes and sizes drifted gently through the channels with the tide. As if this scene weren't grandiose enough, it was duplicated upon the mirror-smooth surface of the sea, broken for an instant by the wispy plume of a blowing humpback whale.

But when I set foot ashore, expecting to delve further into an utterly pristine environment, I found myself stumbling among heaps of twisted cables, rusted tin cans, nail-studded boards, slabs of concrete, and any amount of other refuse. Weddell seals were sleeping near the edge of an oozing patch of black sludge, leaking from a large pile of decaying fuel drums. Gentoo penguins, reclaiming what had for eons been their undisputed territory, fed their chicks amid broken bottles, even using some of the shards, unknowingly, to supplement their pebble nests. Collapsing buildings, boldly painted with the national colors of this long-abandoned

A family of chinstrap penguins poses in the foreground, with gentoos to the rear, at Paradise Bay, Antarctic Peninsula.
(TDR)

base, rattled in the wind. Almost adding insult, a faded Virgin Mary presided over the scene of dereliction from her painted concrete altar. Only the resourceful sheathbills hopped about, using piles of empty barrels as luxury apartment buildings.

What right, I asked myself, do we humans have to force ourselves so arrogantly upon this land and the other living beings with whom we share our planet? And for what reason, scientific or otherwise? As I grew more familiar with Antarctica, I slowly became aware that Paradise Bay was far from an isolated case. From Hope Bay at the Antarctic Peninsula's tip to Cape Hallett in the Ross Sea, to the even more distant shores of Terre Adélie in western Antarctica, penguins had been or are still being ruthlessly evicted for the sake of scientific research bases. If we cannot maintain an element of respect for wildlife in the wildest region on earth, even in the name of science, how can there be any hope anywhere in this world?

Winter Dreams

Humans in Antarctica can only ever be transient. Some may stay for a few hours, others for months or even years. There are tourists, scientists and politicians, mountaineers, explorers, and adventurers. Poets, writers, and artists have visited the great white continent. Whether hunting whales, killing seals, testing a nuclear power plant, netting krill, or organizing an international ski competition, all were, or are, passing. Visitors. The Argentinians once temporarily moved their seat of government to Antarctica and flew in a pregnant mother to produce the first Antarctic citizen. Still, they all move on. Even those few humans each year who elect to spend the long dark winter in Antarctica do so only in tiny elaborate shelters constructed specifically to create a microclimate adapted for humans. Antarctica will never be fully tamed, and it is perhaps this raw power of her wildness that etches itself most deeply upon the emotions of those who visit her.

With winter in the air, I sailed away from Antarctica late one February, like most others, after a few short months blessed by her purity. The night shrouding the peninsula was deep and black, a harbinger of ever shorter days ahead. A lone iceberg, a growler, bobbed languidly in our wake. The wind, though raw, harbored no sound. Already much of the wildlife had departed, and more was soon to follow, all heading north in pursuit of light and life. Low black clouds scudded by and obliterated the last couple of stars. Then a single penguin cry, sharp and questioning, rose from the invisible wavetops. It was the last Antarctic sound I would hear that season.

Now I was left to dream. Dreaming of this land I thought I had come to know, yet knew so little, a land I loved, but in which I would forever remain a stranger. I thought of the magnificent emperor penguins who, unlike all other mobile life forms moving north at this time, were preparing for their journey deep into the Antarctic winter night. The only bird on earth that may never set foot on land, they would soon begin to head south, across numerous miles of sea ice, to newly frozen bays near the southern shores of the continent. Here, with the last light of autumn fading, each female would lay a single huge egg, then leave again for the distant open sea. Bearing the hope for the future of his race through the heart of bitter darkness, for two long months each male would sit with the egg carefully balanced on his feet.

Watching the last hint of jagged mountains recede, wrapped in my down parka, I tried to imagine these birds enduring temperatures of minus 50 degrees centigrade and lower. And a new dream was born: someday, I hoped, I could move south along with the emperors of the ice and

somehow survive by their side through the long winter night. I would like to be with them when they huddle together against the biting cold, see the chicks hatch, and watch the males manage to produce enough food from their crops for them before the females return from the sea. I would be there as the goggle-faced chicks began to grow their new feather coats, and finally when the summer thaw would take the fast ice, and the entire rookery with it, back to sea. Perhaps then I might feel a little more like I belonged in Antarctica.

Gentoo penguin silhouettes stand out against a shredded sunset at Port Lockroy. (TDR)

(Overleaf)

For thirty years New Zealand mountaineers have taught a series of survival courses near Scott Base for both New Zealand and U.S. personnel. By familiarizing researchers with the equipment they will use in the field and imparting basic mountain travel skills, these courses have helped maintain a low accident rate among field parties. Mount Erebus, some forty kilometers away, provides a dramatic backdrop for the courses. Strong wind clouds capping the volcano remind participants how savage the weather can be. (CM)

A full moon sets over Ross Island as the
midnight sun casts soft pink and mauve
hues across the snow, lighting up the
southern flank of the active volcano
Mount Erebus (3,794 meters) about
forty-five kilometers away. The contorted
ridges of sea ice in the foreground jut
skyward, as the McMurdo Sound sea ice
and the Ross Ice Shelf grind against the
island's frozen shoreline. (CM)

Beyond the Stained-Glass Sea

Vignettes from Ross Island and the Transantarctic Mountains of Victoria Land

Crouched among steaming sulphur-crusted fumaroles on the main crater of Mount Erebus, I can sense supernatural forces at play. Up here, high in the thin cold air, powerful magic surrounds this volcano. To me, Erebus has always been the Ice Dragon.

When Erebus stirs, the dragon awakens from the slumbering spell of winter. It is as if her torrid breath has scorched the two-meter-thick sea ice shimmering along the Victoria Land coast. Off the northern edge of Ross Island, near Cape Bird, a mosaic of ice floes jostles for position. The crazy-quilt patchwork grinds together—crunching, overturning, splitting, moving inexorably into the jaws of the Ross Sea. Another Antarctic spring is on the move.

Across McMurdo Sound, the bulky ice-clad peaks and burnt-orange sandstone spires of the Transantarctic Mountains dominate the horizon. Some, such as the 4,000-meter giants of the Royal Society Range, seem to dwarf even Erebus. Over broad piedmont glaciers, past icefalls that flicker in a kaleidoscope of morning light, lie the entrances to the Ferrar, the Taylor, and the Wright valleys. These mystical Dry Valleys float through mirages of quivering ice. The watercolor skyline is brushed with pastels from Edward Wilson's palette—frosty lavenders and turquoises of a newborn polar day.

Resting gingerly on the coiled knobby tip of the dragon's tail, known as Hut Point Peninsula, are New Zealand's Scott Base and the United States' McMurdo Station, two large science administration centers. Big though these bases are, and in spite of crystal-clear air, they can barely be seen from my perch some forty kilometers away. Scratched on the sea ice out from the base complex is the pencil-thin line of the runway that handles cargo planes lumbering south from New Zealand during the short austral summer. Beyond that again, the volcanic dome of Mount Discovery stands as a sentinel, guardian of the passage south.

When you can see past a gilt-edged dragon
to the miracle of frosted leaf
Or when you cringe as cold sheds a tear
yet remain in awe at soft mauve motif
You will have guessed our reason for coming
to an island between Heaven and Hades
Hovering near delicate water
Erebus . . .
Fiery weaver of a stained-glass sea

Erebus summit camp, December 1978

Hurtling down the icy slopes of Mount Erebus toward Cape Royds, these huskies become exhausted and dispirited by poor visibility and wind-driven snow that stings their eyes. One dog handler stays out in front to provide direction for the team while the other steadies the sledge from overturning on sastrugi ridges. (CM)

Wind sears the cold into my bone marrow. With my face mask covering frosted nose and cheeks, watery eyes squint behind smoky-gray goggles. Through fluttering breath, I look along the backbone of Ross Island. The craggy summits of mounts Terra Nova and Terror glow a muted pink as a low-swinging sun skips across the snout of Minna Bluff. In their heyday these dormant neighbors of Erebus formed a snarling, smoldering, multi-headed beast. Ranging between one and five million years old, the volcanoes of Ross Island and Mount Melbourne further up the Victoria Land coast are comparatively young on the geological time chart. Regions such as Marie Byrd Land in western Antarctica contain truly ancient volcanoes. Locked in the grip of the polar plateau, they are now at peace with themselves. Some of the younger ones, however, simmer beneath the ice—waiting.

The Antarctic is ringed by fire. Although Erebus, at 77.5 degrees south latitude, is the southernmost of active Antarctic volcanoes, many of the far-flung subantarctic islands such as Heard, Marion, and Bouvet exhibit various levels of vulcanism. In 1775 Captain Cook discovered the South Sandwich Islands on the eastern fringe of the Scotia Sea. At least eight of these eleven islands contain fumaroles or hot ground, or have actually erupted. Further south toward the Antarctic Peninsula, Deception Island in the South Shetlands is extremely active. After major eruptions in 1967 and 1969 the British and Chilean bases were abandoned due to extensive damage by ash. Today's visitors to Deception's sunken

caldera regularly bathe just off the beach in seawater heated by submarine vents.

At the scaly scree-covered base of Mount Terror lies Cape Crozier, where, in the cruel midwinter darkness of 1911, Edward Wilson from Scott's expedition led a desperate foray in search of an emperor penguin egg, thought then to be a key link in studies of evolution. The vast Ross Ice Shelf, butting into Ross Island at Crozier, is commonly compared to the size of France: it is 300 meters thick near the sea and even thicker inland. Seawater flows beneath it all the way to the foot of the Transantarctic Mountains, only 600 kilometers from the geographic South Pole. The whole shelf rises and falls about a meter to the slow rhythmic breathing of each tidal cycle. This movement, combined with the relentless buildup of pressure from glacial ice feeding down onto the shelf from the plateau, results in the calving of icebergs. Massive tabular bergs shear off, unleashed into the chaos of the Ross Sea. In October 1987 one berg

A New Zealand dog handler enjoys a pipe outside his polar tent before turning in for the night. The "Kiwi dogs" curl up in the snow behind the sledge after a hard run from Scott Base. The saturated midnight colors on Mounts Erebus and Terra Nova give an impression of warmth, whereas the true temperature hovers around minus 40 degrees centigrade. (CM)

measuring 36 by 154 kilometers broke away from the Ross Ice Shelf near the Bay of Whales. The mass and momentum of Antarctic ice shelves such as the Ross, the Filchner, and the Ronne are truly awesome.

Directly below my stance on the crater rim, some 200 meters down vertical crumbling walls, a molten lava lake hisses and heaves. Bubbles of bright red magma mushroom through black shriveled skin only to burst, sending shards of lava over the tattered lip. Groaning, ingested in slow circular swirls, magma is sucked downward again into the volcano's central core. Without warning, once or twice each day, an innocuous-looking vent beside the lava lake glows and then spits fiery fragments hundreds of meters into the air. Molten bombs spatter the main crater floor and at times fly over the rim toward our camp. Each explosion deafens, chilling the soul. Erebus is no ordinary mountain. Without question, the dragon bewitches all who journey south into the heart of the Ross Sea.

I first became enamored with Erebus in 1973, while working at Scott Base as a mountaineer running a series of three-day survival courses for scientists and support personnel. As I cut snow blocks for improvised shelters, practiced cramponing in the icefall, or sat quietly on the veranda of our A-frame chalet, Erebus assumed her dragonlike form and became my mentor. The shape of the plume winging its way south, the patterns of light flitting among crevasses on the upper flanks, and the ever-changing curves of wind cloud arching over the summit caldera etched their way deep into my spirit. Erebus's mood became my mood. The infatuation intensified that year as I traveled to Windless Bight, to White Island, and over the sea ice to capes Evans and Royds. Erebus, during her somber brooding days, brought inner peace and humility when the whole mountain became a ragged tapestry of wind-worn grays.

From 1975 to 1978 I took part in three volcanological expeditions on Erebus. Despite extensive geological survey work in the Transantarctic Mountains throughout the sixties by both U.S. and New Zealand scientists, little detailed work had been done on Erebus. Although the volcano was right on our doorstep, helicopters were not powerful enough then to operate safely around the summit plateau. Even today, with twin-engined machines, flying onto Erebus requires reduced payloads and experienced pilots wearing oxygen masks.

Erebus is one of only three volcanoes in the world with a persistent lava lake (the others are Nyiragongo in Uganda and Erta Ale in the Afar territory of Ethiopia). These semipermanent lava lakes are fundamentally

(Opposite)

Almost fully molted, these Adélie penguins wander along the edge of the sea ice at Cape Royds, trying to summon the courage to leave the rookery for a winter among the pack ice in the northern Ross Sea. Mount Erebus towers over this most southerly breeding ground. (CM)

Most people acknowledge that they will never see penguins in the wild. But just knowing that they are there is enough.

FRANK S. TODD
The Sea World Book of Penguins

As the sun sets over the Transantarctic Mountains on the other side of McMurdo Sound, Adélie penguins prepare to leave the Cape Royds rookery in search of food in the Ross Sea. (CM)

Throughout the breeding season from October to February, the Adélie penguins from the rookery at the southern end of Franklin Island enjoy watching the midnight sun transform their world into a kaleidoscope of burnt-oranges and turquoises. The British navigator James Clark Ross landed on Franklin Island in January 1841, naming the island after Sir John Franklin of the Royal Navy. (CM)

different from the pit lava ponds typical of Hawaiian volcanoes, in that their persistence suggests a direct connection to the magmatic reservoir beneath the volcano. They are the closest scientists can come to actually observing the process of gas and heat transfer and crystallization occurring in a magma chamber. For political and logistic reasons Erebus is by far the most accessible of the three volcanoes.

Following the discovery of the Erebus lava lake in 1972, a joint New Zealand-United States-French expedition in 1974 began probing the defenses of the inner crater. Scientists were keen to make use of Erebus's unusual position and structure by attempting a chemical analysis of gas emissions. Samples would provide knowledge of the earth's mantle from a continent far to the south of other volcanological studies. Understanding how magmas degas is an important factor in learning more about why and how volcanoes erupt. Although some data had been obtained from gas vents on the walls of the main crater, interest mounted in col-

lecting uncontaminated samples from fumaroles tucked away in the inner sanctum beside the lava lake. In 1974, 1976, and 1978 world-renowned volcanologist Haroun Tazieff flew to Antarctica to help New Zealand scientists Phil Kyle and Werner Giggenbach assess the danger, modify sampling techniques, and refine the direction future Erebus research should take.

Progress was slow in an environment dominated by cold, noise, and confusing swirls of unbridled gas and steam. Greek mythology defined Erebus, the son of Chaos, as a personification of mysterious darkness in the underworld of Hades, and it was the ancient Greek philosophers who postulated the need for a southern landmass, Terra Australis Incognita, to balance the known lands in the north. A primordial fear of treading unknown, trembling ground lingered among all of us who came to Mount Erebus. The psychological barriers and logistic hurdles faced by the early Erebus field teams of the seventies proved formidable.

Adelaide Island is a large mountainous island just south of the Antarctic Circle toward the base of the Antarctic Peninsula. The British Antarctic Survey now operates Rothera Base on the southeastern end of the island, following the closure of their old Adelaide Base due to crevassing on the runway. (CM)

(Opposite)

Parent Adélie penguins leap from floe to floe, scuttling back across the sea ice toward the rookery and their chicks at Cape Royds. A small tabular iceberg is grounded against the shoreline of Ross Island. (CM)

Wind in the Antarctic dictates human activity. When temperatures hover around minus 40 degrees centigrade, wind certainly cannot be treated lightly. Living in tents is never easy on Erebus. As a result of the earth's thinner atmosphere at high latitudes, the effective altitude of the volcano is significantly greater than its 3,794 meters would suggest. Gaining height rapidly in a helicopter, combined with dehydration caused by insufficient snow for drinking water, takes its toll on daily work output and health. With symptoms akin to severe altitude sickness, several Erebus workers have needed medical evacuation over the years. It is now mandatory for researchers to spend a few days acclimatizing at an intermediate camp before proceeding to the summit.

In 1975 our acclimatization camp was on Mount Terror. Scattered around the summit, fist-sized nodules of olivine crystal sparkled from boulders of jet-black lava. Sitting by the tent door on calm evenings we could watch cloud shadows dance across the Ross Ice Shelf toward Crozier. The following year, from a campsite at the top of Fang Glacier on the northern side of Erebus, four of us traversed the spine of Fang Ridge, a jagged remnant of an ancient caldera rim. Below, mottled sea ice in Lewis Bay appeared as a vast cathedral window. Little did we realize then that just a few years later the sanctity of Lewis Bay would be shattered by an aircraft accident, the greatest tragedy in Antarctic history.

I still grin when I recall a day trip in 1978 with mountaineer Carl Thompson. We clambered up from the Fang camp to the summit plateau,

This group of inquisitive emperors has waddled across the sea ice at Cape Evans to inspect a New Zealand field party that was visiting Captain Scott's 1910–14 expedition hut. It is refreshing to be regarded by animals in the Antarctic as a curio rather than an object of terror. (CM)

The volcanoes Erebus and Terror dominate this aerial view of the Ross Island skyline. Mount Terra Nova is the slight dome midway between Erebus and Terror. The saddle between Terra Nova and Erebus is 1,610 meters above Lewis Bay, which is located on the far side of the mountains. The 1979 Air New Zealand DC-10 hit Ross Island at 440 meters above Lewis Bay. (CM)

keen to pay a surprise visit on a team of American construction workers finishing off an orange plywood hut in a hollow under the crater rim. After a stiff climb, we circled round the summit ridge, then crept unseen down the scree toward the carpenters toiling away on the roof. Thinking themselves alone on the mountain, they didn't look up from their private world. Hidden behind fumarole towers some fifty meters from the hut, we took off all our clothing except bright yellow mukluks and then bolted toward the hut, whooping like Apache horsemen. Halfway to the hut I crashed through the hollow roof of a cave formed by hot gases escaping under the summit slopes. I tore a knee on volcanic glass and razor-sharp slivers of Pele's hair, and my leg streamed with blood. Undaunted, on we charged. Startled, one carpenter couldn't believe his eyes and nearly fell off the roof. As we naked Kiwis burst through the door, our own faces undoubtedly mirrored the stunned amazement of the woman who had been, unknown to us, busy sealing walls inside.

This hut proved a real boon to Erebus research. No longer did seismograph batteries have to be kept functional by carrying them down ladders and embedding them in the warm soil of underground chambers. Microscopes could now be used to begin on-the-spot taxonomic identification of various species of algae growing in the red-brown heated ground around the crater's flanks. Significantly, the hut became a kitchen to improve cuisine, as well as enabling adequate amounts of snow to be melted for hot drinks.

Low evening sun glistens on the wind-polished ice of the Taylor Glacier as geologists relash equipment onto their wooden sledge. Each sledge carries about 500 kilograms of camping and survey equipment. The rubber tracks on the motorized skidoos are fitted with metal cleets to enable them to grip the iron-hard ice. Windshields are essential to help protect the driver from gales hurtling down the glacier from the polar plateau.
(CM)

Evening skiing around the summit caldera brought lasting memories. On one jaunt, five of us edged our skis across iron-hard sastrugi below the camp. Brushing over velvety patches of frost crystals, we skittered down to the band of fumarole towers overlooking Hut Point Peninsula. The serrated margin of the Erebus Glacier Tongue, which thrusts into Erebus Bay between Cape Evans and McMurdo, glinted in filtered sunlight as a roller coaster of clouds flowed over McMurdo Sound from the south. We hacked a hole in the base of a twenty-meter ice tower formed by condensing steam. It was a relief to escape the keen breeze by crawling inside the chimneylike structure, burying ourselves in hot clammy soil. Although one reeks of sulphur afterwards, such polar saunas are definitely hard to beat. Sheer luxury! When we stepped outside again, however, our moist outer garments instantly froze into suits of armor. Clanking like rusty gates, we huffed and puffed our way back to camp. Wrapping chilled fingers around mugs of hot chocolate brought smiles to glowing faces as we snuggled deep into our down bags.

Just prior to Christmas 1978 the decision was made to attempt to sample gases from fumaroles beside the lava lake. After days of abseiling (rapelling) with packs full of equipment down to the edge of the inner crater, I was finally ready to test the rope system by disappearing below into a cauldron of steam. Despite their vulnerability to heat, we decided to use conventional nylon climbing ropes—a winch with steel cables had proved too heavy and awkward during the 1974 expedition.

On the summit of Mount Erebus. (CM)

I tugged on my gas mask, adjusted the harness, and clipped into the rope. Eyeing the lava lake some 120 meters below, I braced myself on the crumbling rim. Remembering the Chink's comment from the book *Even Cowgirls Get the Blues,* "the man who feels smug in an orderly world has never looked down a volcano," I stepped off.

An excerpt from my diary:

Drop rapidly down double ropes. Lots of loose rubble before reaching total commitment on overhang of pink glassy kenyte. Zip downwards to land on steep yellow ice—panting hard. Thankfully, no tangles. Continue abseiling, then tension-traverse sideways over boulders and rutted gullies—the warm glow of lava. It is eerie to have the lava lake just there in front of me. Keep a watchful eye on the active vent. Take two quick photos, then descend another icy band. Surprised how firm the ice is so near to molten lava—wish I had worn crampons for balance. The rope is not long enough, stopping twenty meters above the floor of the inner crater. However, I am now on easy ground and the way is clear to traverse across to the fumarole Werner wishes to get samples from. Bulbous meringues of dirty yellow snow cluster around me—everything seems to vibrate with the constant roar of escaping gas. Do I have the right to leave footprints on such sacred ground—to be here at all so close to the pulse of the dragon? Can this Jules Verne journey, treading a tightrope between ancient ice and heaving liquid rock, really be in the Antarctic? Fear grows with the sense of trespass. My job done, I radio to be hauled out.

With ash pouring onto my helmet, into my eyes, and into every gap in my clothing, I bounced through the overhang to land like a flapping fish—gasping and haggard—underneath Carl, Harry Keys, and Bill McIntosh, who had been operating the "Z-pulley" crevasse rescue system. I wandered around dazed, had a swig of rum, and then tried to de-ash myself. After changing a frayed rope for a longer one, Werner loaded his titanium rods and gas sampling bottles into his rucksack and set off.

My diary again:

Werner descends smoothly; however, he pauses near the bottom to untangle the new abseil line. Without warning, an enormous eruption shatters the air. Haroun had often said that his fear of being hurled by rapidly expanding gas during

Werner Giggenbach commences his roped descent toward the molten lava lake in Mount Erebus's inner crater. Titanium gas-sampling rods extend from Werner's rucksack, ready to attempt collecting gas from fumaroles beside the lava lake. (CM)

Bright red bubbles continually form in the Erebus lava lake only to burst, sending shards of molten magma over the lip. The magma swirls around under the vertical cliffs of the inner crater and is subducted back into the core of the volcano. (CM)

an eruption was greater than his fear of being injured by flying magma. It is an incredible blast—Werner must be dead! Dozens of spinning molten missiles corkscrew high above us, seemingly in slow motion. Some thud down out of the sky while others hurtle between us, low and fast. Most are about the size of a teapot; however, some very much larger. Mesmerized, everyone somehow manages to dodge the bombs raining around them—Phil Kyle and Kathy Cashman fall over as if in a trance. Bombs poured into the main crater floor to send up hissing geysers of steam as they melt into the snow. With a loud poof one lands right beside the belay rope I am holding. Little time to think but amazed we seem to have emerged unscathed. Werner replies weakly to my desperate call on the radio. Panting, with long, drawn-out pauses between words, he relays that he has been hit on the knee by molten magma! Fortunately, he managed to brush it off quickly with his leather gauntlet before it burnt through his clothing.

Werner badly wanted to push on toward the vents that he had spent years trying to reach. He finally gave in to our pleas to come up, for we strongly suspected the ropes could have been damaged by the heat blast. Humbled by the events of the day, we solemnly trudged out of the main crater. Just as we hauled ourselves up the last section of rope to the crater rim, another crippling blast hewed us to the ground. We cowered behind rocks as brown ash billowed skyward. Our last remnants of bravado collapsed as bombs strafed the entire main crater floor. Our hair matted with ice and ash, our clothes disheveled, we lurched down the scree to camp, feeling resoundly whipped. Beaten, yes, but spiritually charged from a brush with the rawest of elements in this primeval polar world.

Christmas dinner on Erebus was a fun affair. A leg of lamb smothered in vegetables had been wrapped in silver foil and cooked for two days in the hot soil of the side crater. A dozen people ripped into the feast, with Haroun's sweet rum from Martinique providing suitable lubrication. Overhead, reminiscent of Captain Scott's officers' mess at Cape Evans, hung a motley collection of personalized sledging banners. Celebrations were interrupted shortly afterward when Ray Dibble's thirty-kilogram pyramid tent blew away, sending us scurrying into a maelstrom of blinding powder snow to search for his precious sleeping bag. As the wind thrashed us to and fro, holding down bent poles and relashing unruly canvas to anchors became an exercise in temerity. Once again, Erebus had brought good people together.

No one has since dared return to the inner crater. Perhaps that is the way it should be. Nevertheless, Erebus science has moved forward. An elaborate network of seismographs crisscross the caldera, sending contin-

It was easy to see that here, nature was at her mightiest.

ROALD AMUNDSEN

171

At almost 5,000 meters, the summits of Vinson, Shinn, Tyree, Epperly, and Gardner in the Ellsworth Mountains are the highest peaks in Antarctica. In 1935 pioneer American aviator Lincoln Ellsworth sighted the northern part of these mountains during the first transcontinental flight. The highest peaks were first seen in 1957 by a U.S. Navy aircrew that was flying a reconnaissance mission for an International Geophysical Year traverse party. (CM)

ual signals of tremors and eruptions to the Scott Base laboratory. Solar-powered video cameras also beam in graphic views of the lava lake. Biologists, too, are extending their research on both Erebus and the steaming ground of Mount Melbourne by probing further into the curious origins and life cycles of thermophilic organisms.

The recent creation of Sites of Special Scientific Interest (land areas with special rules for access, designated by the Antarctic Treaty nations) in warm ground around the summit plateau should help protect the simple vegetation, as well as minimize the introduction of foreign micro-organisms. Thankfully, in line with the long-standing policy to remove all garbage and human waste from the mountain, awareness has grown for the need to minimize the presence of marker pegs, old cables, and painted rock cairns. This is a problem that urgently needs to be addressed all over the Antarctic.

In a further attempt to understand the volcano's chemical makeup and to compare trace elements with those found in the snow near the South Pole, scientists are using highly refined sampling devices to collect gases. The equipment is mounted inside U.S. Antarctic Program *Hercules* aircraft, which then make repeated passes through the plume. The amount of chlorine emitted from Erebus has recently been estimated by this method. Apparently the chlorine/sulphur ratio of Erebus is abnormally high, which possibly means Erebus is contributing a substantial amount of chlorine to the Antarctic atmosphere. As chlorine is the culprit in the formation of the ozone hole over Antarctica, Erebus the ice dragon could well prove to be a vital link in furthering our understanding of the impact that manmade pollutants such as chlorofluorocarbons are currently having on the earth's protective skin.

From the summit ridge of Brunhilde Peak in the Asgard Range above the Wright Valley, the midnight sun lights up the distant sandstone and dolerite towers of the Olympus Range. New Zealand's Vanda Station lies in the bottom of the Wright Valley between the two mountain ranges. In the valley directly below the climber, the patterned ground of snow-filled, frost-heaved polygons provides a reminder that this landscape is a true polar desert. (CM)

173

No Latitude for Error

On November 19, 1959, New Zealand lost its first person in the Antarctic. A heavy tracked Sno-Cat slammed down a crevasse on the Shackleton Coast some 470 kilometers south of Scott Base, killing one man and destroying the legs of another. Ten years later to the day, the second New Zealander died, this time in a helicopter fire in the Dry Valleys. On November 19, 1979, nothing happened. Nine days later, however, an Air New Zealand DC-10 aircraft on a 9,000-kilometer, eleven-hour sightseeing flight with 257 persons on board plowed into Ross Island just above the ice cliffs surrounding Lewis Bay. No one survived.

When the DC-10 hit, Scott Base had only just wound down the biggest logistics management nightmare New Zealand had ever conducted in the Antarctic, a subsea drilling operation in McMurdo Sound to help geologists date the uplift of the Transantarctic Mountains. It was a confusing, stressful time for all. That Scott Base and McMurdo leaders held the DC-10 recovery operation together while continuing to run their bases for the rest of the summer season is a considerable credit to the strength and unity of the combined New Zealand/United States system in the Antarctic.

As field operations officer for the New Zealand Antarctic Research Programme (NZARP) from 1975 to 1983, the safety of all New Zealand-

Rippled like crumpled cardboard, a slow-moving glacier front hangs over the sea ice of Moubray Bay in North Victoria Land. Cape Hallett is the site of the combined United States/New Zealand science base that was operational throughout the 1960s. A serious fire finally caused the abandonment of the base in the early 1970s. It was not for another decade that pressure increased on the governments to clean up the decaying buildings and bulk fuel drums rotting slowly on the beach. (CM)

Storm clouds gather over the Ross Ice Shelf near Cape Crozier. (CM)

ers working in Antarctica was my responsibility. It was inevitable that I should become involved in the Erebus recovery operation as NZARP mountaineers and surveyors, air accident investigators, New Zealand police, Air New Zealand staff, DC-10 engineers, and New Zealand Face Rescue mountaineers gathered at Scott Base ready to move onto the mountain.

Compared with working on the summit of Erebus, the DC-10 crash site, at only 440 meters above Lewis Bay, could not have been easier. For the most part it was calm and surprisingly warm, with only one spell of extensive fog creating dangerous flying conditions for the McMurdo helicopter crews supporting us. Everyone who flew to the crash site had to come to grips in their own way with the enormity of the tragedy. Clement weather certainly helped those who were in awe of coming to the Antarctic for the first time.

(Overleaf)

The oranges and mauves from a low sun light up the dry powder snow dancing across the McMurdo Sound sea ice. The 3,000-meter volcanic dome of Mount Discovery looms in the distance. (CM)

There is no denying that the personal trauma was immense. It was at least some consolation that many of the mountaineers involved had worked professionally in the Southern Alps of New Zealand and so had dealt to some degree with accident victims. But never had any of us seen death on this scale—complete and utter devastation cutting a swath through this realm of harmony and tranquillity.

The most difficult thing to cope with in a land of perpetual sunlight was pacing ourselves. We had no way of gauging how long it would take to find the voice recorders, track down navigational documents scattered by the wind, survey the site, collect cameras for photographic evidence, and finalize body recovery. There was no darkness to soothe the eyes and mind. Forcing people to rest and to drink adequate liquid was not easy. It was a good move when I asked Eric Saggers to take over the kitchen tent in an attempt to meet the irregular demand for sustenance as workers came off the crash site. Aviation kerosene soaked the snow for an enormous distance, and rather than search for uncontaminated snow it was more efficient to ask for insulated drums of water to be flown in by the helicopters that were removing the bodies. I still have trouble when I smell kerosene at airports.

We survived by outwardly making light of the situation. The mountaineers whistled or sang songs as they worked with the police body-recovery teams. We slid down the slope on plastic bags and even initiated a team effort to roll one of the aircraft's enormous tires over the ice cliff into Lewis Bay. I'm sure this frivolity benefitted some of the younger policemen. Champagne from the First Class compartment helped, too.

My time beside the human wreckage was spent quietly in introspection. I hummed Joan Baez tunes—"Diamonds and Rust." I dwelt on the life of a friend who was a passenger and now lay crumpled in the snow. I remembered her joyous laughter years before, when she woke from a bivouac near the summit of Mount Cook. We had looked down on New Zealand's Westland National Park to buckled glaciers, to fast-moving clouds, to ferns upon ferns upon filigreed ferns. She had loved this coast where only wildness, wind, and wetness reign.

My mind flashed back to when I had come down from the 1978 Erebus expedition. U.S. aviators had just returned exhausted to McMurdo, having flown their ski-equipped Hercules completely across the continent to rescue a badly injured Soviet aircrew. It felt good to be involved in a place where if a mishap occurs anywhere on the continent there are no questions asked, no drums beaten, and no dollars counted. There is simply the best possible attempt made to mount a rescue. It meant a lot to work in an environment where ownership and wealth from exploitable resources were not dominant issues, where there were no accepted national boundaries, and where militarization and the dumping of nuclear waste were prohibited. Such sanity would benefit the rest of our fragile, frightened world.

I pondered the direction of my own life and my dire need to step sideways from the senseless scurry and worry in which the western technological world had immersed me. I wondered what constituted an acceptable level of human involvement with the seventh continent. What effects have resulted from both science and commercial activities? Why cannot more garbage, unwanted material, and abandoned buildings be removed on transport that often heads north half-empty? Surely, the dreadful mistakes made in the Arctic must not be repeated here. What lies ahead? Mining? Never!

My commitment to the absolute necessity of minimizing human impact in Antarctica, and for the retention of the polar and mountain regions as wilderness, stems from this emotional period. Following the Air New Zealand crash, it was natural that the word "Erebus" should conjure visions of horror and destruction in the minds of the New Zealand people. New Zealand is a small, tight-knit community, and a great many families were affected in some way by this tragedy. Even now, more than ten years after the accident, the shroud from Erebus is just starting to lift.

I have not returned to work on the volcano. Recently, though, it has been a great joy to make three voyages to Ross Island from South America on tour vessels such as the *Lindblad* (now the *Society*) *Explorer.* On one voyage, after an exciting ten-day cruise from the Antarctic Peninsula, we were able to nudge the ship toward the Ross Ice Shelf near Cape Crozier. As the wind ripped across the edge of the shelf, fingers of cold, talcumlike snow spiraled from jagged ice cliffs, shrieking into the sky above the *Explorer.*

The wind dropped as the *Explorer* sailed into Lewis Bay. We approached a cluster of tabular bergs, pockmarked with iridescent blue caverns etched into the marbled ice by wave action. Around the base of the bergs, snow petrels with cheeky charcoal eyes darted to and fro, their sleek white bodies skipping across the tops of waves. Dwarfed by the immensity of the bergs, these birds appeared minute yet were totally in control on this boundless pewter sea. The paradox of such frailty thriving in a harsh, uncompromising environment confirmed that tiny seabirds like the snow petrel and the dancing Wilson's storm petrel perfectly embody the Antarctic's purity and vitality. To then see Erebus materialize through sea smoke from a wind-flecked Southern Ocean was a moving, sentimental moment for me—like coming home.

As the little red *Explorer* pulled away from Ross Island and set a course for Cape Hallett, the water became coated in a greasy slush of frazil and pancake ice—the first indication that winter was clamping around the continent. Golden swells heaved and sighed in slow rhythmic motion as our bow sliced northward. The night was far too beautiful to spend in my bunk. I stood for hours on deck watching the backlit ocher curve of Erebus gradually merge with a colbalt sea.

Four expeditions in the early 1900s had used Ross Island as a gateway to the interior and, for the brave, the South Pole. The headquarters for the Scott and Shackleton expeditions from 1901 to 1917 were wooden huts constructed on the black volcanic beaches below Erebus at Hut Point, Cape Evans, and Cape Royds. Crunching over the rough scoria in front of these bases, I can almost still hear the cheery shouts of Englishmen in woolens and windproofs, committed to the task ahead.

Erebus provided companionship as they lived and toiled in the shadow of the dragon's plume. These Edwardians were not used to the sense of wonder big mountain environments can stimulate. Erebus's impact comes through strongly in the official accounts of these expeditions, but even more so in *The South Polar Times* and *Aurora Australis,* beautiful books handcrafted under the mountain itself. As Apsley Cherry-Garrard, a member of Scott's 1910–13 expedition, recorded in his time-honored book *The Worst Journey in the World:*

I have seen Fuji, the most dainty and graceful of all mountains; and also Kinchinjunga; only Michael Angelo among men could have conceived such grandeur. But give me Erebus for my friend. Whoever made Erebus knew all the charm of horizontal lines . . . and so he is the most restful mountain in the world, and I was glad when I knew that our hut would lie at his feet.

The familiar shape of the volcano was also a guiding beacon, a welcome sight as weary sledging parties returned from depot-laying epics across the monotony of the Ross Ice Shelf. The quest to reach the geographic South Pole dominated their thinking (as it has most subsequent polar literature). Of late, it has been popular to castigate Captain Scott as an inept leader, a somewhat poor organizer of expedition logistics when contrasted to the professional Amundsen. While this criticism may have substance, the quality of various scientific investigations initiated around the base of Erebus by Scott and Shackleton should never be forgotten or underrated. Similarly, the sledging trips to the fringe of the Dry Valleys, to Crozier in winter, and to the South Magnetic Pole are far more significant to me than the journeys toward the geographic Pole. The struggle to be first at the Pole was driven by inflated egos and the promise of

The Splendid Burning Mountain

A New Zealand dog handler pulls out a thermos flask for a hot drink while his huskies rest on the terrace in front of Captain Scott's 1910 headquarters. The design of modern kit-set wooden sledges tied together by cord and rawhide has not changed since the turn of the century.
(CM)

military promotion; in some respects, it was little more than a flag-waving exercise to fan the embers of a fading British Empire. These pioneering battles with the environment were also grand adventures. They should be seen and simply accepted as such. Their power to inspire has stood the test of time.

Six members of Shackleton's 1907–9 expedition led by Douglas Mawson and Professor Edgeworth David made the first ascent of Erebus from Cape Royds in March 1908. A team of Scott's men under scientist Raymond Priestley completed the second ascent in December 1912 from Cape Evans. These parties recorded the first basic scientific observations from the summit region. Their man-hauling escapades, which involved holding down tents in frightful storms, the agony of frostbitten fingers, and being caught in eruptions, are commonly remembered as the earliest encounters with the volcano.

A wind cloud forms at sunset over Cape Evans, providing a dramatic backdrop for Scott's 1910–13 hut and Barne Glacier. (CM)

In my view, though, Erebus belongs to an expedition that approached Ross Island fully sixty years before the Shackleton/Scott era. James Clark Ross is perhaps the least known of all the British Antarctic explorers. Between the ages of eighteen and thirty-eight Ross spent no less than seventeen years in the Arctic. He was undoubtedly considered the British officer of his day most capable of leading a seaborne expedition in polar regions. Following his attainment of the North Magnetic Pole in 1831, he was a natural choice to command an expedition bound to venture beyond the misty extremities of the map toward the South Magnetic Pole. Ross's provisioning and outfitting of his vessels *HMS Erebus* and *Terror* was without question the best in British polar experience.

Early in the New Year of 1841, Ross's efforts to reach the magnetic pole in these sturdy converted warships were thwarted by the discovery of high ice-clad mountains along the Victoria Land coast. The pole lay tantalizingly out of reach—inland beyond 4,000-meter Mount Minto. Had Ross ventured to the region today, because of the nomadic swing of the magnetic poles he could have sailed directly over the exact spot, now located off the coast near the French station Dumont d'Urville.

Ross pushed south, finally breaking through pack ice into the mighty sea that now bears his name. On January 28 he recorded the first sighting of Erebus in his journal:

It proved to be a mountain twelve thousand four hundred feet of elevation above the level of the sea, emitting flame and smoke in great profusion; at first the smoke appeared like snow drift, but as we drew nearer, its true character became manifest. The discovery of an active volcano in so high a southern latitude cannot but be esteemed a circumstance of high geological importance and interest, and contribute to throw some further light on the physical construction of our globe.

And later, having named the two principal peaks after his vessels, he wrote:

At 4 p.m. Mount Erebus was observed to emit smoke and flame in unusual quantities, producing a most grand spectacle. A volume of dense smoke was projected at each successive jet with great force, in a vertical column, to the height of between a hundred and two thousand feet above the mouth of the crater . . . Whenever the smoke cleared away, the bright red flame that filled the mouth of the crater was clearly perceptible; and some of the officers believed they could see streams of lava pouring down its sides.

Blacksmith Sullivan, a member of Ross's crew, simply called Erebus "This Splendid Burning Mountain." I would gladly trade all my Antarctic travels to have stood on the deck of *HMS Erebus* beside Sullivan that day.

Strangely, apart from a brief landing on Franklin Island, Ross never came ashore directly under Erebus. He did, however, sail eastward for over two weeks, discovering the "Great Barrier," later named the Ross Ice Shelf. The full story of Ross's voyages is worth reading as one of the most delightful and gripping in all the polar literature. In 1912 Roald Amundsen wrote of Ross:

Few people of the present day are capable of rightly appreciating this heroic deed, this brilliant proof of human courage and energy. With two ponderous craft—regular "tubs" according to our ideas—these men sailed right into the heart of the pack, which all previous explorers had regarded as certain death. It is not merely difficult to grasp this; it is simply impossible—to us, who with a motion of the hand can set the screw going, and wriggle out of the first difficulty we encounter. These men were heroes—heroes in the highest sense of the word.

So much has changed in the Antarctic since Ross hammered his vessels south into unknown waters. Periodically we all have an intrinsic need to experience some form of wildness not possible within the confines of modern living. Today travelers can voyage to the Ross Sea in tour vessels simply to rejuvenate the spirit. Such cruises remain expensive, seemingly for the privileged few; some visitors, though, sell everything they own just to visit an untamed land for a few precious weeks. These people have told me their sacrifice has been amply repaid merely by sighting their first iceberg.

Ross Island, with its battered expedition huts still weathering storms under Erebus, provides visitors with a particularly moving and tangible link to the Antarctic pioneers. Such an evocative connection with the early exploration of a continent cannot readily be made elsewhere. Many visitors aim—through on-board lectures and constant questioning of staff, but mainly through their own sensory experience in places like Cape Evans—to open magical new doors in their quest to learn something of polar history. Such people return to the Antarctic again and again. After thirty years of activity, seaborne tourism in Antarctica remains a highly educational experience. Properly controlled, with sensitive leadership on suitable vessels, its impact on the environment should continue to be minimal. Visitors exposed to the Antarctic in this way are becoming a powerful, positive influence capable of promoting protective measures to retain Antarctica as true wilderness.

Dog Power

"The long drawn-out yowl from a husky," I wrote in my diary in 1979, "pawing the air while he strains at the limit of his chain, settles deeply in the bones. Early October on Ross Island is always a magical time. The snow is so cold and dry it chimes like tiny hammers on fluted glass as yellow mukluks prance among the dogs being harnessed. Smiles spread, each of the dog handlers is as eager to be away from Scott Base as the yelping huskies."

Perhaps the most passionate aspect of the ten summers I spent in Antarctica with the New Zealanders was working with the huskies, better known at Scott Base as "Kiwi dogs." Each year I was responsible for ensuring that the new dog handler received adequate training both in New Zealand and during the month-long transition ("hand-over") period with the outgoing handler. There were many things to cover, ranging from veterinary instruction to the idiosyncrasies of breeding dogs with a severely restricted gene pool. Repair work on the fleet of wooden sledges and maintenance of other vital field equipment that clutters up an Antarctic base were key elements, too. The climax of the hand-over periods was the sledging trips we had with the dogs. These mini-epics taught lessons about Antarctic travel no instruction manual could ever cover.

Dog teams from Scott Base played a crucial role during the sixties in geological and survey mapping reconnaissance work in the outer reaches of the Transantarctic Mountains. One journey during the 1963–64 summer notched up 2,500 kilometers. Unlike the British, who remained almost totally dependent on dog power until 1975, in part due to weaker crevasse bridges and rotten sea ice on the warmer Antarctic Peninsula, New Zealanders began experimenting with "tin dogs" or skidoos from the mid-sixties onward. Arguments raged for years among pundits about the benefits of each mode of travel, with quips such as "You will always get home with a dog team" or "You can't eat a carburetor" being commonplace banter in the Scott Base bar.

By the seventies, Kiwi dogs were only used as short-term support for science parties working close to home around Ross Island or on the Ross Ice Shelf. The huskies did continue, however, to be the focus for recreational activities with base personnel. Sadly, in 1987, New Zealand threw away the best public relations tool and outlet for pent-up emotions

Oblivious to blizzards driving across the McMurdo Sound sea ice, the Scott Base huskies survive quite happily by tucking their noses under their rumps. The snow is so dry it squeaks like polystyrene when walked upon, making it difficult to sneak up on a sleeping dog. (CM)

En route to Cape Royds, a New Zealand dog team clatters over the slick two-meter-thick sea ice under the plastic-looking Barne Glacier. The Barne sweeps off the flank of Mount Erebus between capes Royds and Evans. (CM)

it ever had in the Antarctic: the Kiwi dogs were given to the American Will Steger, who had already driven his dogs to the North Pole. Five Kiwi dogs, however, completed the south-north traverse of Greenland with Steger in 1988 in preparation for his Trans-Antarctica 1990 International Expedition across Antarctica by its longest axis.

It was fitting that some of New Zealand's noble huskies should return to the continent for one final fling. Yet the huskies have outlived their usefulness for government operations in Antarctica. It seems likely that, when Britain, Australia, and Argentina phase out their last few animals, dogs will figure in future Antarctic history only in the domain of private adventures.

I long to have experienced the era of the extended New Zealand dog journeys, yet am pleased to have enjoyed a decade of at least some association with Antarctic dog travel. Each of the hand-over journeys will live with me always. Excerpts from my diaries on three of the trips best

express the mood and the memories. From a 200-kilometer round-trip across McMurdo Sound into the heart of the Royal Society Range:

Every item has to be packed with care on a dog sledge. It is partly the necessity for this precision which makes the sledging experience, akin to climbing, so deeply satisfying. Con, the new "doggo," is introduced to Pete's routines and after a vicious spat between two highly strung bitches quickly learns the importance of harnessing compatible dogs to the main trace at just the right moment.

We romp out into the McMurdo Sound. How good it feels to replace the constant hum of the base's generators for the almost audible hum of silence inside my balaclava, and the metallic scrape of a bulldozer blade for the occasional scruff-squeak-scrape of a wooden sledge runner on sea ice. Six hundred meters of muffled sea moil beneath this icy skin.

Even the huskies are limp and chilled as we creep onto the Bowers Piedmont at the Strand Moraines on the far side of the Sound. Once their fatty pemmican blocks are gulped down they curl quickly, burying noses into rumps. It is a cold, shadowy camp.

The snouts of our double-down bags are frozen by morning, though sizzling bacon soon sees twitching noses nuzzle through the halo of rimy breath.

It is a long uphill grind across the rutted piedmont. The three of us often have to lend shoulders to the load or guide the front of the creaking sledge between twisted sastrugi to avert capsize. To enter the Blue Glacier as 3,000-meter-high walls of the Royal Society peaks rise over eleven wagging tails is electric.

In 1979, every route on the seaward side of the 4,000-meter Royal Society Range was untouched. I returned one month after this dog trip with a geological party and climbed two of the sweeping ridges, Hooker and Giulia. My partner, geologist Adrian Daly, lost parts of several toes and fingers to frostbite. On a spring journey to Cape Crozier, I wrote:

October 24th—We slip quietly away from Scott Base with fifteen dogs. Our lead dog Hansen had died of a heart attack in September following a cold strenuous pull across McMurdo Sound from New Harbour. As we get deeper into the featureless Windless Bight the new lead dog becomes disoriented. Gary and I take turns to ski in front of the team, grateful we had hot-waxed the skis and sledge runners. A perfect day on velvet-smooth powder snow, though face and hands remain cold despite two balaclavas, three pairs of gloves, and continuous exertion.

Camp is pitched thirty kilometers out in the center of Windless Bight. Once the dogs are spanned and fed I photograph soft evening light on Erebus. One film shatters with the cold and my fingers are soon wooden and near useless

(Overleaf)

The New Zealand huskies are the most southern of all dog teams in Antarctica. Despite the harsh conditions and long dark winters, they do not need to be kept inside or in kennels. During summer these dogs are tethered on the sea ice in front of Scott Base and later moved to the edge of the Ross Ice Shelf. (CM)

*from trying to adjust the tripod. Painful thawing hands bring tears. Fried sal-
ami and strong black coffee laced with honey lure me inside the polar tent.
Wriggle into a double-down sleeping bag cradling a VHF radio and frozen
gloves. Doggo's scented baccy fumes curl towards the apex of the tent, mingling
with mittens and balaclavas hung up to dry. I drift off, watching flames from
the setting sun lick skyward through the folds in the circular entrance.*

*October 25th—A Hercules on a low-level training mission circles above
us, dipping its wings. The twelve kilometers of superb skiing in front of the team
towards Cape Mackay encourages the dogs to pull the sledge with renewed vigor.
They rumble at my heels like fifteen rasping drummers on hollow crusty snow.
Hugging Cape Mackay to avoid crevassed pressure ridges, a wall of mist skuds
across the Ross Ice Shelf to wrap silver fingers around Erebus and Terror. We
are soon enveloped in eerie fog with an ice halo forming around a feeble colorless
sun. Fall asleep on the sledge only to be jolted awake moments later by a husky
licking my face. Consume dark chocolate to find energy for the icy-fast skiing to
Crozier. Camp beside the remains of Wilson's stone igloo—occasional snowflakes
shimmy from a dove-gray sky. A smashed box, a bamboo pole, strips of frayed
canvas, a ball of twine, and a bedraggled emperor [penguin] carcass lie embedded in translucent ice—grim reminders of the "Worst Journey" retreat to Cape
Evans some seventy years ago.*

In October 1980 four of us contrived an attempt to get two dog teams to
the summit of Erebus following a run from Scott Base along the coastline
to Cape Royds:

*The sledge room, the most memorable haven in Scott Base, smells strongly of
linseed oil, blubber-stained anoraks, old sweat, and damp dog hair. Our plans
change dramatically when "Bad Jelly" puts a chisel through his hand while
stripping rawhide sledge lashings. The decision is made to drop one of the dog
teams (you have to be careful where you drop a dog team or it gets upset!),
resorting the equipment to suit a threesome. Despite pruning all nonessentials,
the extra weight of the sledge is to significantly influence our eventual movements on the mountain. . . .*

*Weddell seals bask beside a crack in the sea ice. They suckle doleful new-
born pups. Taking care to give the seals a wide berth we scamper onto the little
snowy beach in front of Scott's hut. Although we only stay long enough to rest
the dogs, it will remain a precious visit to Cape Evans. There is not a mark
on the silken protective layer of winter snow which forms a lacework over the
roof. Velvet-gray snowbanks buttress the walls. Towering storm clouds frame
whalebone-white canvas and scoria-blasted wood. No one approaches the building. No one speaks. The dogs, too, sense the peace within and sit on their*

Manhauling sledges in the Ellsworth Mountains: not an easy task. (CM)

(Opposite)

Climbers attempting Vinson Massif, the highest peak in Antarctica, haul all their equipment toward the base of the Ellsworth Mountains in fiberglass sledges. Although Vinson is not a technically demanding climb, mountaineering in Antarctica is a serious undertaking requiring proper logistic support, well-thought-out food and equipment, and a team capable of operating in high winds and low temperatures. (CM)

haunches, whimpering softly. We lean on the sledge parked on a wind-scooped terrace above the front door. Only hot chocolate splashing into the thermos mug disturbs the silence. If only Scott had had these dogs . . . suddenly the raucous caw of a bunch of Antarctic clowns startles us. Twenty inquisitive emperor penguins waddle towards bristling huskies. . . .

Then later, above Cape Royds:

It is a long tiring day battling uphill towards Erebus. A constant southerly nags our windproofs, slowly but surely sucking away energy and the ability to think clearly. It worries the dogs, too, and they will not turn into the peppering drift no matter how much encouragement is given.

After only five hours on the move, with our altimeter registering barely 600 meters, we are forced to seek shelter. Progress towards the mountain is discouraging—the true scale of Erebus is driven home. To our dismay the wind strengthens. Despite a frantic search there is no alternative but to accept that we are caught in the open with no hope of a lee slope to hide from the rising ground storm. Blue sky above taunts. One by one whining huskies are tethered to a chain stretched between a dead-man anchor hacked into the ice and a lava outcrop. I attempt to break up the surface with a shovel so the dogs can dig in. However, I soon give up as I am losing valuable energy trying to control the flailing shovel in the wind, energy I will desperately need for the real test ahead—erecting the tent.

Every piece of equipment unlashed from the sledge has to be secured somehow, for one casual action and in a flash it will be gone. We crawl on hands and knees placing ice screws and humping large rocks for the tent guys. A climbing rope is clove-hitched around the apex of the tent and, while one belays, the other two struggle to raise the polar pyramid into the gale. It takes four buffeted attempts before we are brave enough to let the poles go and commit the straining nylon to the array of anchors. A lightweight climbing tent would not have survived this tempest for more than a few seconds. Strong wind is frightening—really frightening. To lose the polar tent now would put everything on the line.

While the others sort the sleeping gear and commence battle with the primus, I tension the sledge between two ice screws, double-checking the security of the remaining load. Lurching about the camp, I am continually knocked down by powerful gusts, bruising shins. I clutch an ice ax, as the danger of being blown away is very real. I am painfully aware my shouts to the others are rapidly beginning to sound slurred. This whole terrifying maneuver of securing the camp has taken fully three hours to complete. Elbowing through the tunnel entrance I am greeted by steamy bearded smiles offering hot chocolate. . . .

McMurdo Sound sea ice buckles as it grinds into the edge of Ross Island near Scott Base, causing three-meter-high pressure ridges to be created. Melt pools form between the ridges, allowing Weddell seals to nuzzle their way through the ice to make breathing holes. It is around these holes in the October/November spring months that the Weddells give birth to their pups. (CM)

Twenty-four hours later the storm blows itself out. After sledging further up the mountain the dogs are left at 1,800 meters just below Hooper's Shoulder and I scramble to the summit plateau of Erebus by Priestley's 1912 route. The draining effect of a rapid climb to altitude makes this an exhausting excursion, however nowhere near as taxing as the speedy descent with the dogs back to Cape Royds. . . .

Sledging down, the polished rutted surface is slick and treacherous though metal keels and rope brakes on the runners slow us sufficiently to ensure survival. A thick rising sea fog engulfs us. The run towards the Sound with a full load is the most stressful yet exhilarating sledging of the whole journey. The southerly strengthens again, smothering us in powder snow and making it awkward to control the dogs. Judging distances in the whiteout is deceptive and nerve-wracking. We become jittery about hurtling over the ten-meter ice cliff encircling Backdoor Bay. The lead dog, a fuzzy ball of matted, ice-clogged hair, peers at us over his shoulder seeking courage and direction in the swirling murk. . . .

Licking and nibbling iced-up, bruised paws, the weary dogs are left to rest on the sea ice while we clamber over the snowed-up headland to Cape Royds. Swaddled in down jackets with hoods pulled sharply across our faces, it is a slow mechanical approach to the ghosted outline of Shackleton's hut. As I wade through a meter-high snowdrift a very irate Adélie with flippers thrashing the snow suddenly squawks into the air. At 77.5 degrees south, Royds is the most southerly penguin rookery. As we look towards the sea cliffs, hundreds of Adélies cower, facing bleakly into the wind, each desperately trying to huddle over eggs as snow packs in tightly around them. At times, even penguins have a tenuous grip on life this far south.

Shackleton's 1907–9 expedition base is the most inspiring shrine in Antarctica. Stepping into the heroic glimmer, I remembered another wild night here when I crept away from camp to curl up on the floor. Musty smells of rusted iron and reindeer sleeping bags pervaded the drift of my mind, creating images from the many happy evenings this little cabin has witnessed: pipe smokers yarning, jolly pantomimes, rhubarb pie, with candles under the Albion press to keep the ink from freezing; Joyce and Wild working long into the night in the "Rogue's Retreat" to print pages for Aurora Australis; *"Nemo," the Boss, writing his Erebus poem, "Keeper of the Southern Gateway, grim, rugged, gloomy and grand. . . ." I was rocked to sleep that night by wind worrying the hut— the bleached timbers creaking and groaning just as the old Nimrod would have done punching into the Ross Sea.*

Turning for home, that brief respite from the storm keeps me warm for the next five hours as we slog into a stiff southerly back to Scott Base. . . . Now I know these dogs will be dogs, these greatest of dogs, but I wish they wouldn't pee on my windsuit. Sleep well!

A husky waits for the next journey, beneath a wind cloud at Cape Crozier.
(CM)

To the Driest Edge

From a distance there is simply a black line. Then another, and set in creamy yellow mudstone on the rim of a cliff three more. Stone logs sleek as ebony and rippled ringlets of stumps lie snapped and scattered by the casual whim of time. This is the fossil forest on Mount Fleming at the head of Wright Valley, one of the Dry Valleys of Victoria Land that displays the patina of footprints from the dance of the continents.

Wildcat flurries of wind claw us, ripping past in irascible katabatic turmoil. The madcap frenzy of chilled air cascades from an eyrie birthplace on the polar plateau into the Labyrinth and on down its hurried way to McMurdo Sound. The petrified remnants at our feet appear withered, polished into preservation by the wind's freeze-dried fury rather than merely trapped by the callous crush of sediment. Cold stone wood.

Prince Edward kneels, running his fingers over the raised surface of an ancient tree. I squat beside him, my back to the wind. Yelling through cupped hands I describe how Antarctica was once much warmer, permitting the growth of lush vegetation such as fernlike *Glossopteris,* which thrived in low-lying swamps. *Glossopteris* fossils had been found in the tent beside the bodies of the ill-fated Scott party in 1912. Dr. Wilson had not abandoned them even when faced with his own demise. They proved to be similar to those already discovered in India, South Africa, Australia, and South America dating from the 270-million-year-old Permian epoch. This precious cargo was the first direct evidence later used to corroborate Antarctica's past union with other continents.

Forty million years went by before the flora of the Triassic evolved, covering parts of the continent with *Dicroidium* ferns and beech and conifer trees such as those now laid bare on Mount Fleming. The vast majority of Antarctica is presently hidden under ice, so it is fortunate for scientists that fossils are accessible here in the Dry Valleys and on peaks such as those above the Beardmore Glacier. The fossil record of both plants and, significantly, vertebrate animals provides the proof scientists need to confirm the existence of the ancient supercontinent Gondwanaland.

It is exciting for Prince Edward to flick switches in the Antarctic time machine and touch traces of a bygone world. Earlier in the day, on this royal tour of Ross Dependency, we had flown to Beacon Valley, an offshoot of the Taylor Glacier, to witness the result of the accumulation of all this carbonaceous material. At the base of sandstone pillars, coal seams several meters thick split wind-blasted walls of yellow rock. Low-grade by present commercial standards, coal is readily found throughout the Transantarctic Mountains. As we returned to the helicopter I tried to imagine the herbivorous swamp-dwelling reptile *Lystrosaurus* and its cousin the carnivorous *Thrinaxodon* roaming a land that had not yet witnessed the spectacular rise of the alpine peaks around us, let alone the evolution of volcanic Ross Island.

A significant proportion of the United States/New Zealand Earth Science Program in Antarctica over the last two decades has been dedicated to drilling projects in the Dry Valleys and in the deepwater sediments of McMurdo Sound. Dating the dramatic upthrust of the Transantarctic Mountains has been an important element in understanding the continent's glacial history. In providing a direct linkage with the past, Antarctic glacial geology will continue to reveal key factors affecting present world climate change.

(Opposite)

Dolerite, largely carved by wind, forms fantastically shaped ventifacts scattered throughout the Dry Valleys of Victoria Land. Some are smooth and sharply angled pyramid shapes, while others are pitted and honeycombed by both wind and salt erosion. Behind this meter-high ventifact on the northern side of the Olympus Range can be seen the head of the Balham and Barwick Valleys, a pristine valley system designated as a Site of Special Scientific Interest. (CM)

The orange helicopter sways on its haunches like a dragonfly balancing on the tip of a flower. Leaving wind-blown Mount Fleming, the U.S. Navy pilot peels the machine over the cliff, plummeting toward the Asgard Range that skirts the southern fringe of Wright Valley. It is only a fifteen-minute flight to the New Zealand base Vanda, where a traditional Kiwi lunch of vegetable soup and fresh-baked scones is served with lashings of tea. Although researchers from all over the world tend to congregate at Vanda, it is not every day a hungry young prince drops in out of the sky. Approaching the Vanda oasis for lunch, Prince Edward is greeted by the cardboard clatter of washed woolens hanging stiffly on the line. A frozen pair of long johns crackles from the flag pole, while a mummified seal looks on with disdain. Optimistically, the mail box contains two empty milk bottles. An aroma of hot buttered scones wafts through the kitchen door as we take off heavy yellow parkas in the porch.

Vanda Station has been described as snug, solar-powered, spartan. Built in 1966, it is normally operational from late October to the end of January. The Kiwis have also wintered over there on three occasions. The base is a collection of plywood boxes perched on a terrace beside Lake Vanda as if stuck there on an architect's cutout model. The pod of pea-green huts is glued in position against the wind by cables frozen into holes drilled in the permafrost. Workers can almost set their watches on the afternoon arrival of the gravity-fed katabatic wind.

Field parties descending to Vanda for a break and cleanup after weeks of roaming the hills always arrive smiling. Coppery cheeks are burnished by wind, and lily-white lines slice across necks where parkas begin. Leathery brown fingers are gnarled and cracked by dryness. Dust is impregnated in unkempt hair, and the wild light of the mountains shines in their eyes. The glazed, faraway look after opening well-fingered letters from home, the ribald radio exchanges with others still in the field, and the carefree chatter with rum flowing long into the night remind me of Orwell's passionate vagabonds in *Down and Out in Paris and London*. The sense of freedom generated by an unbounded expanse of eroded rock and sky intensely affects anyone who lingers here.

Back in 1973 I worked with an Italian expedition in the Dry Valleys. Prior to a riotous Christmas at Vanda, Himalayan veteran Ignazio Piussi and I climbed the virgin west face of the Obelisk, a prominent sandstone pinnacle in the Asgard Range. Homeward bound in the softness of evening, Ignazio and I cramponed down the south ridge. A sudden burst of light caught the crests of the thin lines of snow trapped in frost-heaved grooves honeycombed on the rocky ground. To me, the symmetry of the

(Opposite)

The 3,794-meter volcano Mount Erebus is dwarfed by the immensity of McMurdo Sound. Newly formed sea ice catches the autumn sun. Soon, as early March approaches, temperatures will plummet and winter will grip Ross Island. (CM)

To anyone who goes to the Antarctic, there is a tremendous appeal, an unparalleled combination of grandeur, beauty, vastness, loneliness, and malevolence—all of which sound terribly melodramatic—but which truthfully convey the actual feeling of Antarctica. Where else in the world are all of these descriptors really true?

CAPTAIN T. L. M. SUNTER
in The Antarctic Century newsletter

(Opposite)

A pyramid berg and mountain scenery converge near the entrance to the Lemaire Channel. (TDR)

checkered polygons girdling the Obelisk's snowy turrets took polar mountaineering into the hazy realm of fantasy.

The Obelisk was the first of several new climbing routes in Ross Dependency over the next decade. It had been an Australian Boy Scout journal that spurred me as a youth to emigrate across the Tasman Sea and work with the New Zealanders in Antarctica. Magazine accounts of Sir Edmund Hillary's private Antarctic expedition to climb the elegant Mount Herschel in North Victoria Land in 1967 and American ascents the year before of the continent's highest summits in the Ellsworth Mountains also had a major effect on my aspirations as a young mountaineer. Climbing in the Ellsworth Mountains near the base of the Antarctic Peninsula in December 1988 fulfilled a twenty-year dream. Standing on Vinson Massif, the closest point on the earth to the widening ozone hole, and looking into the heart of the Ellsworths, I was further convinced that the mountains of Antarctica will be one of the great meccas for climbers in the next century.

The grace and grandeur of Antarctica's big peaks and the ineffable seclusion of the Dry Valleys have altered the course of my life. I once found scratched on a wall at Vanda part of a quote by a New Zealand mountaineer, the late Jill Tremain: "What a privilege to know the profound stillness and peace of the land. . . ." Had Jill ever been to the Dry Valleys in another lifetime? Does she bide there still?

The Onyx River, the largest in Victoria Land, flows inland from a coastal ice piedmont to Lake Vanda for a few weeks each summer. Viewed from cliffs in the Olympus range, it resembles a silent silver trickle, slowly wending its way up-valley. Sweepstake fever runs high at Vanda and in seedy bars on Ross Island as to when the Onyx will actually make it to the stream-gauging weir on the lakeshore. Sometimes the Onyx loses heart halfway and perishes in choking drifts of sand and stone. In flood, it has provided a helter-skelter raft ride for a zany band of Kiwi desperadoes called the "Asgard Rangers." By monitoring the Onyx, lake levels throughout the valley system, and the movement of hanging glaciers draped on screes like discarded slippers, the Asgard Rangers help keep tabs on imperceptible fluctuations of local climate change.

To walk the frozen surface of Lake Vanda is to journey with Alice in Wonderland. Prisms of ice, four meters thick, form a looking glass into the purest water on earth. Perfectly still, yet receiving the sun's energy through the lens of ice above, lake water becomes progressively warmer as density and salinity increase with depth in distinct stratified layers. It is 26 degrees centigrade on the bottom at seventy meters. Primitive algae

lurk below, gradually forming thick, slimy mats on bottom sediments. In limbo above, trapped in surface ice, conical sprays of bubbles blossom, uncurling toward the sun. In spring, Lake Vanda's ice is cold and dry to the point that it is sticky, virtually impossible to skate on. In Don Juan Pond near the Labyrinth, the water is so saturated with a unique mineral salt—antarcticite—that even in winter at minus 60 degrees centigrade it does not freeze.

Littered here and there across the landscape, wayward crabeater and Weddell seals have humped inland to die alone, far from the compassion of the sea. Some of these vagrants have squirmed as high as 700 meters into the hills before food reserves and stamina succumbed to the bite of the wind. Rainless centuries have mummified their blubbery hulks; their parched, opalescent stares trouble passing visitors.

To the casual observer, life in the Dry Valleys has been pared beyond recovery—snuffed out. Not so. Ephemeral streams straggling from glacier snouts are brought to life by sunshine, with emerald-green flushes of algae gleaming in the brightness of summer. Nearby, lakeshores reveal a crinkled, desiccated algal scum that has gradually surfaced through the ice. The majority of lichens are dull gray, yellow, or black, though some are more gaudy, ruddy, and rough. Welded to granite boulders or tucked away in tiny exfoliated cracks, they can imbibe moisture from a mere skerrick of snow. Flat, crusty, not daring to raise their heads to the wind, most are not the luxuriant foliose varieties found on the Antarctic Peninsula. The cunning endolithic lichens avoid the wind altogether. They eke out a furtive existence inside the structure of rocks, hidden beneath the first few crystalline layers. For plants stripped to bare essentials, with water and light in extreme shortage for much of the year, their grip on life is admirably tenacious.

For many travelers in these parts it is the rocks themselves that come to life. Ventifacts—carefully crafted by wind and salt erosion—the dolerites, granites, and sandstones are transformed into fantastic creatures that change shape with each fresh glance. Squirrels, elephants, and hobbits abound. Their simplicity of form, smoothness, and sensual curve demand that they be touched. The mood of the rocks alters, too, as a skiff of snow blows in from the polar plateau. Other creations evolve as snow disappears, not melting but sublimated to water vapor, essentially evaporating before your eyes into the sky across the driest edge. Truly this is Tolkien country—a vale of 10,000 runes, an Entwood of stone. Walking in the Dry Valleys, one is never alone.

A strict code of ethics exists here concerning the removal of waste products. Field parties must take all garbage, including human waste, directly back to Ross Island or at least to centralize it at Vanda for subsequent export from the Dry Valley ecosystem. Sadly, for years most of this waste was jettisoned onto McMurdo Sound's sea ice. In an attempt to stop the lasting damage caused by vehicles in the Dry Valleys, the only one permitted today is a ramshackle Ferguson farm tractor dating from Sir Edmund Hillary's jaunt to the South Pole in 1957–58 in support of the Commonwealth Trans-Antarctic Expedition. It now hauls equipment between Vanda and the helicopter pad a hundred meters away.

The environmental impact assessment for the Dry Valley Drilling Project of the early seventies was the first of its type in Antarctica. It wasn't perfect, but it led to a tightening up of attitudes regarding the environmental impact of other science programs. The potential for construction of excessive numbers of science/refuge huts in the region also needs review, while marker pegs, rock cairns, and other experimental aids should be dismantled and removed at the conclusion of each project. It is commendable that the crashed helicopter which for many years was a hideous eyesore in the lower Wright Valley has now been sawn up and removed.

Constant vigilance is necessary to ensure that policies relating to the Sites of Special Scientific Interest scattered throughout the Dry Valleys are respected. Some sites such as the Barwick Valley, which is a prime example of an extreme polar desert ecosystem, require particularly careful management to avoid the introduction of microorganisms. With no surface vehicle or aircraft access, scientists may only enter the Barwick after a long walk from the Wright Valley. Continuing this control on activities in the Barwick is necessary to retain the valley's pristine nature both for its own intrinsic value and for the environmental research of future generations.

A Prince at the Pole

Tiny rainbows dance as sunlight catches the icy drift of tinkling prisms. At minus 33 degrees centigrade it is not cold by the standards of this place, but a dry searing cold nonetheless that seeps insidiously into the body, stiffening movement.

The sun is pasty yellow and ringed by feathered halos. An inane chromed sphere on a striped barber's pole mirrors distorted images of Antarctic Treaty nations' flags across the curved desert snow. The reflection from this polished orb, finely balanced at 2,800 meters on the polar plateau, is the ultimate parabolic juncture of emerald sky and ice. From this cluster of meridians every vista is north. How could this lofty grandstand ever be described as "the bottom of the world"?

We are at the geographic South Pole—a hallowed blank on the map for the pioneers of yesteryear, and for the past three decades a priceless scientific window on the upper atmosphere. Below, perfectly preserved in an icy catalog of information thousands of meters thick, is a layered chronology of cataclysmic events ranging from volcanic eruptions to the delinquent debris of our atomic age.

Nearby, like a giant armadillo, squats the geodesic dome housing the United States Antarctic Program's Amundsen-Scott South Pole Station. Not only a pivotal place for science, the South Pole is now a honeypot for hardy travelers. In 1958, coming from opposite sides of the continent, "Bunny" Fuchs and Hillary met in an icy cloud of dogs, farm tractors, and Sno-Cats—the first overlanders to journey here since Scott turned wearily back toward the Beardmore nearly a half century before.

Only twelve teams, whether national or privately sponsored, have made it overland to the Pole. Most, on scientific traverses, have used cumbersome tractor trains. Some have puttered there on skidoos, manhauled unwieldy plastic sledges, and recently one commercial group clattered over the sastrugi on nordic skis with skidoo support. The bureaucratic hurdles faced by these expeditions have often been a stiffer test of staying power than anything posed by the journey itself. Back in January 1988, the Canadian company Adventure Network International flew the first commercial visitors to 90 degrees south latitude. The barriers are down; others will follow. In February 1990 Italian mountaineer Reinhold Messner and German Arved Fuchs completed their ninety-two-day ski journey across the continent from the Ronne Ice Shelf to Ross Island. Two weeks later, in early March, the dog teams of the Trans-Antarctica 1990 International Expedition finally descended from the polar plateau to the Soviet base Mirnyy on East Antarctica's Wilkes Coast. This, the fourth crossing of Antarctica, was a triumph for dog power and international cooperation. The rules for independent private expeditions are well established now. There is no excuse for poor planning.

In December 1982 I accompanied Prince Edward's tour group to the Pole following a three-hour flight from Ross Island across the spine of the Transantarctic Mountains. Although the prince's father, the Duke of Edinburgh, had visited the Antarctic Peninsula on the royal yacht *Britannia* in 1957, this was the first royal visit to the heart of the continent. For the prince it was a rare opportunity to clown by standing on his head in the middle of a featureless plain, and then to mingle with U.S. scientists, asking pertinent questions about their research. He also received a gift of ice core dating from the birth of Christ.

Later that day, Erebus the Ice Dragon glistened in the midnight sun as the *Hercules* droned toward Ross Island. The sea ice was breaking up to the north, with a distant blue-black line of Southern Ocean beckoning. It was time to return home to New Zealand, though I knew once again that, having ventured beyond the stained-glass sea, I could never be the same again.

The Imperatives of Protection

My journeys to Antarctica spanning sixteen years have provided an opportunity to reflect on the future management of the continent. The Antarctic Treaty has been hailed internationally as a great success for the past thirty years. Indeed, it has been. While the basic tenets of the treaty are well thought out and have been largely respected, there is no room now for complacency.

Antarctic Treaty nations have agreed over the years to various conventions that strengthen environmental management. The "Agreed Measures for the Conservation of Antarctic Fauna and Flora" was signed in 1964, the "Conservation of Antarctic Seals" in 1972, and the "Convention for the Conservation of Antarctic Marine Living Resources" in 1980. There is now a push to create an all-encompassing environmental protection regime to carry us well into the next century. We need to control a variety of current problems: the proliferation of bases that, among other things, increasingly compete for space with wildlife; the tragic siting of permanent airstrips amid penguin breeding grounds; garbage disposal from both land- and sea-based operations; and the use of non-ice-strengthened vessels for private expeditions. A revised Antarctic Treaty or a new regime should somehow ban or severely restrict oil and gas exploration or mining on the continent and in the Southern Ocean. The original treaty negotiators never dreamed that miners would look this far south; as we well know, however, this has already been a century of unprecedented change. Some have argued that the time has come to designate Antarctica as a wilderness preserve.

Even in this age of rapid transportation and satellite technology, Antarctica continues to startle us as an inexhaustible treasure trove of basic and, in many cases, vital scientific information. On one front alone, the Antarctic is proving invaluable as a monitor of global climatic change and atmospheric pollution. The recent discovery of a rapid deterioration in the protective skin of ozone in the upper atmosphere over both polar regions has been alarming. A suggested link between a diminished ozone layer and decreased phytoplankton production is very unsettling. Less phytoplankton means less food for krill, and potentially less krill for Antarctica's penguins, seals, and whales. Since scientists still do not know with certainty the exact life history of krill, it is debatable whether the current harvest of both krill and finfish can be considered a fair and sustainable yield or an ecological tragedy.

On another environmental front, Greenpeace established a small base under Mount Erebus at Cape Evans in 1986, funded by growing public concern about Antarctica. Responding to many complaints from both sides of the continent, some Antarctic programs have been jolted out of the lethargy with which they have condoned the disposal of waste products near bases or in the ocean. We should be shocked that streams of gasoline flow into the sea from bases on King George Island, that fresh pond water there in a zone once designated a Specially Protected Area is now labeled unfit for drinking, and that water quality studies in McMurdo Sound also indicate that the seawater is heavily polluted. Journalists often sideswipe private expeditions or tourists arriving at the South Pole who may happen to drop an orange peel or the like. Yet when filing their reports, they conveniently forget to mention that some have dumped indescribable amounts of refuse on the ice cap at Pole Station for years. Discarded products from what I call the "age of plastics" are not only a problem for the Antarctic environment, but serve to highlight the mire of nonrecyclable material we surround ourselves with every day at home.

I still grapple with wild dreams of modifying the Antarctic Treaty to protect the continent as never before. Could we eventually rub out the unrealistic and in some cases overlapping territorial claims on the Antarctic map? Sadly, this seems further away than ever after the 1982 Argentinian-British conflict on South Georgia brought modern warfare to a region Shackleton called the "Gateway to Antarctica." With the dramatic increase in the number of nations constructing bases in recent years, combined with more private expedition vessels, the buildup of shipping in Antarctic waters can only increase the chances of disastrous oil spills. The sinking of the West German *Gotland II* off North Victoria Land in 1981 and the fuel spill resulting from the grounding of the Argentinian vessel *Bahia Paraiso* on the Antarctic Peninsula in 1989 are stern warnings. There is a need to purposely scale down logistic operations, with an increase in the sharing of facilities and a concerted effort toward more international multidisciplinary programs on the continent.

Through efficient use of current technology we could significantly reduce the clutter of our permanent presence in Antarctica, as well as challenge the concept that membership in the treaty "club" requires a substantial scientific presence or the construction of new bases. An improved treaty should reject efforts to bolster territorial claims by military colonization with associated towns, schools, and "home births." Above all, we need to alter our standard of living, so that we can do without the bountiful mineral wealth supposedly sequestered within Antarctica.

Antarctica continues to attract bold dreamers. Whether they come to seek scientific data, to climb mountain summits, or simply to wonder at Antarctic wildlife, all remain transient visitors. They have a very real responsibility to ensure that their conduct is in harmony with the Antarctic environment and its unique flora and fauna. Each of us comes away inspired. We all must help disseminate awareness of the urgent need for the complete protection of Antarctica as wilderness.

This is no longer a time for inept platitudes about conquests and frontiers. Antarctica is on our doorstep and is clearly an integral part of the mechanism that drives and sustains our planet. The pursuit of science through, at times, an excessive injection of logistic support has already scarred the Antarctic. The pursuit of wealth would destroy it. We can still choose to retain the continent simply as "wild ice." In Antarctica, as nowhere else, that opportunity remains within our grasp.

(CM)

Perspectives on Antarctic Photography

Documenting Antarctic expeditions has often pushed me to the limit, way beyond the mental and physical demands imposed by the journeys themselves. Securing pictures that command attention because of high impact and poignancy adds a new dimension to my concept of traveling through remote regions.

The quality of light in Antarctica is stunning. In my opinion it has rarely been adequately photographed. This is in part due to the fact that very few have explored in any depth the vastly different biological and climatic zones of Antarctica with the sole aim of detailed, creative photography. Most photographers still have other primary roles when traveling on the continent, such as supporting science, loading sledges, or battling the wind just to get the tent secure. During action-packed days or merely by the necessity to keep moving, picture-taking is often relegated to the occasional calm period around a campsite at the end of a hard day. A need for warmth or the simple pressure to survive has interfered all too often in my drive for strong images.

Bad weather, however, is definitely the time to take the camera out, not to put it away. I love threatening charcoal skies, iced-up, weather-beaten faces, and driving sleet with penguins scurrying in all directions on a frozen beach. Or somber ebony clouds that polish an ice cliff into a mosaic of swirling grays to remind the pilot, the sea captain, the mountaineer, and the scientist of their insignificance. Mood is vital. An Antarctic photograph is successful if it captures the whipping of the human ego into total submission. Better still are the images that completely lack the human presence; after all, wherever we go in Antarctica we are intruders. Great pictures help remind us of that.

The following comments may be useful to photographers visiting Antarctica for the first time.

Preparations

If you need new equipment, buy it well before departure. Months before leaving for Antarctica familiarize yourself with all camera functions. Put as many rolls through as possible, taking careful note of exposures and the results you achieve in a variety of situations, such as over sunlit water and snow. Get used to moving the aperture ring, focus, and winding mechanism while wearing gloves. Change lenses until you can do it without looking; in the Antarctic you often have to concentrate on where you are placing your feet while you move quickly to get the next shot. Practice the loading procedure until it is second nature.

"Winterizing" new SLR cameras for extreme cold is expensive and generally not warranted. The molybdenum and silicone lubricants used today are sufficient for temperatures down to at least minus 35 degrees centigrade. Older SLR camera shutters may slow down, with mirrors jamming up at excessively low temperatures. Carry spare batteries. This is particularly crucial for modern automatic and autofocus cameras, which chew batteries at alarming rates in real cold. Spare batteries are also important if you plan to use flash or auto-winding mechanisms.

Clothing

Careful choice of clothing should make it easy for you to keep the camera around your neck, ready to use. One-piece windsuits and bib-fronted insulated salopette trousers are ideal for protecting cameras and keeping meter batteries warm. Fiber-pile or down-insulated hand-warming pockets on your outer garment are essential. When the camera is tucked inside the bib, you no longer get bashed in the face as you climb or ski. Do not, however, keep the camera next to your sweaty body, because condensation on the viewfinder can result in aggravating delays.

Photographic gear should not be stored in a day pack; it simply takes too long to find the requisite piece of equipment. An uninsulated waistcoat that has many different-sized zippered pockets dedicated to spare lenses, filters, and exposed and unexposed film is one workable solution. Get into the habit of storing things in definite places so you can reach for them without looking.

Close-weave, synthetic, fingered gloves are a welcome boon for retaining dexterity while handling cold metal. They wear out quickly, so take spares. Keep outer mitts on elasticated wrist loops, so they don't blow away while you are concentrating on a picture. Mitts must be able to be pulled on quickly to rewarm fingers between shots. Heavier outer gauntlets (again with elasticated wrist loops) are often necessary for higher regions away from the coast.

Gear Bags

The most versatile camera bag I have ever used in the Antarctic is a foam-lined "bum-bag" made by Lowe that clips around my waist. When not in use the bag can be swung to the back or side (a normal rucksack can be worn at the same time), leaving my arms completely free. When gear is required, the bum-bag is simply swiveled to the front for ready access to its velcroed, partitioned compartments. Unlike a traditional skier's bag, the Lowe is stiff enough not to flop heavy gear onto the snow when the zippered lid is opened. If my gear doesn't fit in the Lowe bag, it stays behind.

Camera Bodies

I take three OM1 and OM4 Olympus camera bodies on an expedition, on the premise that it is better to have at least one spare at base camp than to attempt repair work in the field. While working with two bodies, the spare is kept sealed in a dust- and waterproof container.

I travel with two bodies around my neck until the strains of high altitude necessitate that one is left behind. To minimize changing lenses, each body is fitted with complementary lenses, often 24mm and a light zoom 75–150mm. In extreme conditions it is convenient to have both bodies containing the same film, giving seventy-two frames before reloading becomes necessary.

I favor SLR cameras with the least amount of electronics, to minimize the effects of cold or rough handling. This explains my preference for sticking to lightweight OM1s. The OM4 has sophisticated metering but virtually shuts down in extreme cold. When the extra weight of an SLR becomes prohibitive, miniature 35mm cameras such as the Olympus XA series are ideal and, with practice, give quality results. A neat-fitting pocket sewn inside a windsuit can house this tiny camera in a ready-to-use position. The flimsy wrist-strap such cameras commonly feature should be discarded and replaced with a nylon webbing neck sling.

Dispense with camera cases (this may save money at time of purchase) and rely on the padding in the bum-bag or salopettes. Cases are a nuisance when changing films in bad conditions. Throw away camera straps, which are usually too long and if plasticized become stiff in the cold. Replace with two-centimeter-wide nylon webbing, a different color for each body. Sew this around the camera lugs so the length will fit just inside the top of your salopettes. Tape spare film cannisters around the strap so you always have some backup if separated from your bulk supply. Tape parts of the camera body likely to come into contact with your face, or you may become stuck on the job.

Auto-Wind Mechanisms

Motor-drive units and auto-winds come into their own for detailed portraiture or capturing wildlife in action. It is fortunate that, apart from zippy skiers, most people in the Antarctic move slowly enough to make a motor drive unwarranted. In extremely low-humidity conditions such as in the interior of Antarctica, care is needed in using a motor drive. With film moving rapidly across the back of a camera, static electricity can produce awful blue streaks and scratches on the emulsion.

Lenses

For cold-fingered camera work, scrap any screw-mounted lenses you still have. Bayonet lenses are a must. I prefer to dispense with lens caps altogether, because they are so fiddly. Instead I rely on a metal (not rubber) lens hood to give protection; it also shields out unwanted light.

My preference on expeditions is for 18, 24, 35–70, 75–150, and 300mm lenses. The zooms add lightweight versatility, aiding composition in tight spots. The 24mm is a favorite, particularly for situations where the subject is extremely close, yet obtaining a sharp panoramic background is important.

Tripods

For polar photography it is hard to strike an acceptable compromise between tripod weight and stability. The decision to carry a sizable tripod is highly dependent on your means of transport. A tripod head that can clamp onto an ice ax is one solution for high-altitude work. Time exposures of moonscapes and the frigid interiors of historic huts are worth striving for despite the discomfort required to capture them. Make sure that the tightening lugs on the legs of a collapsible tripod are sturdy and easy to operate with gloves.

Filtration Keep filtration to a minimum, if for no other reason than that filters are diabolical things to screw on and off with numb fingers. UV or Skylight (1A) filters are useful for screening excessive ultraviolet rays, as well as for lens protection. A split (top half gray/bottom half clear) neutral density filter is often valuable when shooting a dark foreground with a bright background of mountains or clouds: the top half of the filter holds back the exposure of the mountains by one or two f-stops. A polarizing filter (which works to maximum effect at right angles to the sun) can be used judiciously for beefing up watery skies or cutting through haze.

Film Buy film stock well in advance. Never expect duty-free sources overseas en route to Antarctica to have the film type and ASA you require. Unless in a tight spot, do not buy film from an Antarctic base, as it will often have been stored in an overheated building. Remove all packaging at home to cut down on bulk and waste-disposal problems in the field. (All garbage should be removed from Antarctica.) Mark the ASA rating on the film cannister lid with felt pen. Develop a system for recording notes relating to each roll you shoot.

Keep the bulk of your film stock with you as hand-carry luggage on the airplane. Guard it closely from repeated exposure to X-ray machines, some of dubious antiquity in South America. IATA regulations state that you can insist on visual inspection of film and camera gear. Do not be talked out of it.

Rewind exposed film completely into the cannister. Do not leave the leading edge of the film out, or you risk double exposure by reshooting the same roll when confused by altitude or fatigue. Excited or in a rush, many photographers wind and rewind film too quickly. This habit is asking for static electricity discharge marks, which can result in a blue line through the whole roll in dry polar conditions. Film also gets brittle in the cold; sprocket holes may tear unless gentle winding becomes the norm. Always make sure film is advancing smoothly and without crunching noises, which usually indicate torn film. Fine windblown grit is a menace, especially in the Dry Valleys of Victoria Land. It can get inside any camera, particularly when changing films. Clean assiduously between each roll if possible—at least daily with a blower brush for all gear.

Snow Photography There is nothing more boring than overexposed snow scenes, snow texture being all-important to the mood of the picture. In general, I rely on my light meter, but on overcast days snow can appear muddy unless purposely overexposed by one or two stops. Early morning and evening light is usually the most alluring and evocative in the polar regions. If possible avoid midsummer/midday lighting, which usually produces harsh, contrasty pictures. Bracketing exposures for "once-in-a-lifetime" events in tricky light is a sensible approach, though these situations can occur every few hours in Antarctica and film rationing may become a consideration.

When returning into a warm moist tent or building, a supercooled camera will soon be coated in condensation. Make the transition to the warmth a gradual one by encapsulating the camera in a plastic bag before bringing it inside, encouraging moisture to form on the bag instead of the camera.

Holding your breath at the moment of shutter release is often important to minimize camera shake. This is a real chore for the high-altitude or cold-weather photographer, but it rewards perseverance. When powder snow gets onto the camera, do not be tempted to blow it off. Moist breath will freeze instantly on the viewfinder or lens. I carry a small towel to help with this problem.

COLIN MONTEATH

There is a singular moment for which all photographers yearn: opening the slide pack, putting the individual mounts on the light table and under the loupe, then realizing that there are some slam-dunk keepers. Such special images, faithfully recorded on film, make all of the hours of practice and effort worthwhile, but in no way diminish the reality that photography is hard work. Antarctic photography represents a particularly frustrating variety; numb hands and fingers, ice-caked skin, and howling winds make steadiness with the camera fiendishly difficult.

While the four of us coauthors have some clear differences regarding equipment and technique, we likely would agree that our most successful Antarctic photographs come from our hearts and souls, not necessarily from technical prowess and expertise. Photography is a test of conscience: knowing your subject, studying it, preparing your equipment for the show that you hope will erupt before your eyes, and then having more than a fair share of good luck. When dealing with the quickly changing conditions and constantly moving wildlife of the Antarctic scene, there's hardly any time to think. Instinct dominates because there are no setups.

I have a decided preference for natural-light photography. Although fill-flash and polarizing or split-screen neutral-density filters occasionally creep into my repertoire, these moments are rare. My game is stalking and handling, as best I can, the circumstances with which I'm presented. I feel a much greater satisfaction in my having worked a particular situation or a particular animal to the fullest, without causing any disturbance.

I also like to travel lightly. A minimum of gear increases my chances of getting to where I want to go safely, inconspicuously, and quickly. My experiences in the Antarctic have consistently involved rugged circumstances, strenuous hiking and climbing, and often abysmal weather. There's no question that cameras on tripods produce sharper images, and there's little doubt that carrying ten lenses and three bodies at all times maximizes one's chances for having the best equipment at any necessary instant. But since I have never viewed my photography as an all-out endgame, I've moved toward packing fewer and fewer lenses (perhaps only two or three in the field at a given moment) and sometimes a monopod. I rely on certain "money" lenses to cover a range of focal lengths, all of which have large maximum apertures to give me the necessary speed. I have a favorite core group of Canon "L" series optics: the f3.5 20–35mm zoom; the f4 300mm; and recently the autofocus f2.8 80–200 zoom.

My film of choice is Professional Kodachrome 64 slide film (PKR64)—"pro" film because it is not subject to the vagaries of aging on the shelves (although you do have to keep it cold, and use it relatively soon after purchase) and ASA 64 speed because of the tight grain. Regular Kodachrome 64 (K64) certainly works fine in a

Film, Exposure, Composition, and Depth of Field

211

pinch. To my eye, slide film gives me a true representation of the shoot, unmarred by the vagaries and manipulations of the printing process in the darkroom; slides are also preferred by most editors with whom I've worked. I prefer very fast lenses (f1.8 to f4 maximum aperture), so I am not hampered by the relative slowness of PKR64 in dim light; however, Kodachrome 25 is a bit too slow even for my array of hardware and my usual wildlife subjects. Recently I've made some use of high-speed Kodachrome 200, which, despite the increased grain, helps on those extremely dismal days when the albatrosses are flying near at hand. An archival benefit is that Kodachrome is supposed to have 100 years of storage life.

For a two-year period, I shot a good deal of Professional Fujichrome 50 and 100, but have now essentially abandoned them. The greens are too unreal, an especially vexing problem on the Antarctic fringe, where tussock grass abounds. On the light table and under the loupe, Kodachrome looks sharper and more accurate to my eyes.

I tend to underexpose Kodachrome by at least ⅓ to ½ a stop and, if a white albatross or Antarctic snow and ice dominate the viewfinder, by two-thirds of a stop or more. This makes for more color-saturated pictures, and avoids much of the washed-out pallor endemic to Antarctic photos. Without underexposure, the fine details of an albatross's plumage will be lost, as will the details of sastrugi in the snow or wizened shapes and patterns on the ice. But choosing to underexpose requires knowing what basic exposure is suggested in the first place. Because of the Antarctic's excessive whiteness and light scattering, I distrust the exposures recommended by my camera's built-in metering system. All exposure meters are calibrated to a "normal" scene yielding an 18 percent reflectance, approximately equivalent to the reflectance of a black-and-white checkerboard. Too much white or black, however, skews the reflectance; too much white will cause an underexposed picture and too much black will cause an overexposure, as the meter adjusts for these excesses.

I avoid these problems by metering off a handy replacement object that is neutral in tone and calibrated to the necessary 18 percent reflectance. I often check this substitute reading against an incident light meter. My primary substitute object is the palm of my left hand, metered by using the spot-metering capabilities of my camera bodies (Canon T-90, EOS-1, and New F-1). From practice in the field and in varying light, I know that my palm varies from 18 percent reflectance by two-thirds of a stop. I spot-meter my palm in light equivalent to that of my subject; I know that my camera reading will be two-thirds of a stop away from that 18 percent reading, which I can then obtain by opening up two-thirds of a stop (either by increasing the lens opening or decreasing the shutter speed). Another useful substitute is your camera bag, perhaps the only other thing besides your hand that's always available in the field. Light-canvas Domke bags, for example, lend themselves well to this substitute metering technique.

Discovering gimmicks in one's camera also helps. The T-90 has the ability to average up to nine different spot readings, and I find this capacity quite helpful in the field. For example, penguins have much stark black and gleaming white feathering. An average of two spot readings, one in each area, yields the approximate 18 percent reading you'll be looking for as a start, prior to any decision to underexpose.

All said, it's important to bracket an exciting shot when possible. If you've got a particularly appealing scene in view, take a couple of extra shots on either side of the chosen exposure. It's better to be safe rather than to miss a great scene.

If you don't use the substitute approach, and rely simply on your camera's normal metering program (usually called center-weighted metering), remember that too much white or black in the viewfinder biases the meter. Strong white will take your camera's meter reading two or three stops under the 18 percent reflectance reading; the compensation is to open up by increasing the lens opening or decreasing the shutter speed. Strong black will push your camera's meter two or three stops over the 18 percent reading; in this case, compensate by decreasing the lens opening or increasing the shutter speed.

I've had success shooting at all hours and under all kinds of light conditions, from bright sun to dense fog. The problem with midday sun, however, is that glare is emphasized and subjects appear too stark and contrasty. The best times for shooting are therefore early and late, when there are more shadows and lower sun angles that add undeniable spark to one's photos. Even though there are many cloudy days in the Wild Ice, don't put your camera away! The reflectance of light from the surrounding ice and water will allow a special softness to be captured quite easily.

Composing exciting shots is another challenge. I follow some simple guidelines: never place the subject in the middle of the viewfinder, and watch the background carefully. Go for the corners, placing your principal subject toward one of the four edges of the frame. Then make sure that your subject's prominence isn't nullified by conflict in the background. If you concentrate exclusively on the subject, ignoring the background, you're likely to capture stray, out-of-focus material that destroys your intended emphasis. Fast-moving individual subjects usually dictate a fast shutter speed and a large aperture, resulting in a sharply focused subject with a narrow depth of focus. If you're shooting a landscape and want to have a sharp focus on most of the scene, you're going to have to use a smaller aperture and, likely, a slower shutter speed. Use your depth-of-field preview button to ascertain if you've managed to sharply focus the scene in the viewfinder. I am able to handhold my short lenses down to $\frac{1}{60}$ of a second.

Working with Antarctic Wildlife

If you've preset your camera exposure and decided that the light is good for shooting, the only elements still needed are a cooperative subject and your own patience. Be careful of Antarctic fur seals, however. They are quite dangerous, can easily outrun you on the beach, and would love to chomp on your posterior.

Flying seabirds are an undeniable treat of any Deep South adventure, but they require fast shutter speeds and some careful balance while you're on the rocking, rolling deck waiting for them to fly by. I highly recommend the so-called Hosking holder, developed by the great British photographer Eric Hosking, which I have learned from Jim Snyder and Christiana Carvalho. This strategy requires attaching a monopod to one end of your lens, with the other end placed in a flagpole holder slung over your neck and shoulders. These holders, commonly used by marching bands, can be obtained quite cheaply from advertising supply stores. The setup maintains a solid balance on a tossing platform, and frees you to concentrate on your subject.

No matter what the situation, it is critical not to desecrate the Antarctic environment. Keeping a safe distance from the animals and not trampling the habitat is a responsibility of every Antarctic photographer. All Antarctic visitors should never leave plastic or any other nonbiodegradable waste anywhere on the continent or in the Southern Sea, nor should they trespass on protected areas, interfere with research efforts, or take any souvenirs.

RON NAVEEN

Nature photography has been alternately called an art, a means of scientific documentation, or simply work—among many other labels ascribed to it over the years—requiring patience, dedication, creativity, and in-depth technical knowledge. In our case, none of the above applies. To us, photography is quite simply an extension of our desire to observe and remember the ways of nature and its inhabitants, and to share what we have observed and remembered with others. Thus, focusing on a soaring albatross from the deck of a rolling ship is not "work" but a fascinating way of concentrating on an extraordinary bird; waiting all morning to catch a glimpse of a penguin chick just emerging from its egg is not an exercise in patience but an excitingly spent six hours; and dunking an underwater camera between icebergs for a fleeting shot of a diving cormorant is not so much a case of dedication as a thrilling challenge that turns icy water lapping up the sleeves into a mere inconvenience.

We do not set out in search of any particular shot, but rather meander about with little or no preconceived ideas beyond an attraction to some general subject or location, snatching what pleases the eye as it is encountered. That we might make our living from the results is important, but secondary, perhaps like painters who do not take commissions but rather paint at their own whims, only to seek a market later. We do not like the word "creativity," because we do not believe we create anything at all, but simply attempt to maintain a sense of perception sufficiently attuned to our surroundings so as not to miss the moment, sometimes exceedingly brief, when all the components of light, movement, background, and setting come together to render an exceptionally aesthetic view.

Photography can be seen as an acute selection process, the ability to see instantly and decisively which part of an often broad, complicated scene is the most attractive, to recognize which factors make it outstanding and which are irrelevant. By focusing on those factors and leaving out all that is redundant, the quality of the moment may be intensified to capture a mood far stronger than that present in the overall scene. For instance, in the midst of a vast penguin rookery there may be a single ridge where the birds stand out against a pale green mossy slope. Beyond, a deep blue fractured glacier has yet to catch the morning sun. By choosing the right position and lens, this view, at the exclusion of all else, may produce an image far more evocative than the broad one. Another example: when photographing steep mountainsides we sometimes find it more appealing to omit the skyline, giving the illusion that the face rears up indefinitely rather than presenting the true but uneventful shape of the mountain.

Conversely, some visual experiences may be totally impossible to capture on film. These are the scenes whose very character derives from their vastness, where sky and foreground, close-up and distance, deep shade and bright sun all combine to create an exceptionally pleasing impression. We have taken to calling this "a vision that does not fit inside the camera." If photography is an art, then it must be the art of seeing.

We do not like using anything but natural light. The use of strobe or other artificial light completely destroys what we feel is fundamental to nature photography: capturing the mood of natural illumination. Even modern film, however, is incapable of accommodating the range of contrast between brilliant sunlight, especially on snow or water, and deep shadows the way our eye is able to compensate. This is especially true the higher the sun climbs in the sky, and the more powerful its rays. The best hours for photography in Antarctica are often somewhere in between what normal people regard as appropriate for after-dinner drinks and early morning coffee. With the risk of losing the most spectacular moments of the southern summer, when sunshine like liquid gold may splash the face of bergs against inky skies, or the silvery moon is dwarfed by ice-blue peaks, this situation definitely calls for some rearrangement of conventional routine. (Is there anything conventional about Antarctica anyway?)

Lighting

Good photography does not, of course, necessitate sunshine. Heavy, pregnant skies, so dark that snow and ice in the foreground appear to glow in contrast, create some of the most dramatic moods, while thick snowfall, with penguins moving about disembodied in all the whiteness, conveys the special character of Antarctica better than any brilliant sunny day. And simple, dull gray ceilings, while sometimes drab for the broad view, bring out exquisite texture and color shades in close-up wildlife portraits, completely devoid of shadows even at high noon.

Because they have never been molested by any large land predators, most seals and seabirds, if approached with sensitivity and common sense, are extraordinarily unafraid of humans. This produces numerous situations in which you can not only choose the exact angle and framing you might like while the animals go about their lives undisturbed, but also line up appealing foregrounds or backgrounds, or move closer or further away. Where choices of position are freely available we have also found that almost invariably a low shooting angle—at or below eye level with the animal—greatly enhances a feeling of size, life, and dignity in the subject, and allows for more space in distant background. From the more normal—and far more convenient—standing angle we can only capture animals smaller than ourselves, unflatteringly plastered against the nondescript substrate. Needless to say, a guano-splattered photographer is not always the most socially acceptable individual after a long day of groveling on his stomach through a penguin rookery.

For the ease of being able to interchange lenses, we both use Nikon gear, although in practice we rarely do so because so much dependence on each other would severely limit our flexibility of movement. We have also chosen different camera mod-

Gear and Equipment

els, with Mark relying on a Nikon F-3 for its sturdiness, and Tui preferring the lighter but now outmoded Nikon FE-2, because it is the only model featuring the simple, easy-to-use matched needles metering system. Both types enable us to set our exposures manually, which we prefer over automatic mode. For fast action and general wildlife use, we rely on motor drives at all times in the relative warmth of the Antarctic coastal regions.

We each carry six lenses and one body in an attempt to balance minimum weight with maximum flexibility of angles; a spare body is kept as a reserve but is not usually carried in the field. Our lenses, although not identical, cover a range from 18 to 300mm, with a couple of medium zooms in between: Nikkor 32–76mm and 75–150mm. Prized possessions are our Tamron F.2.8 180mm and 300mm, which are excellent for low-light, hand-held wildlife photography. Although higher ASA ratings would sometimes be tempting when light is scarce, we have found that, of the slide films we have tried, only Kodachrome 64 renders with admirable faithfulness the soft textures and delicate shadings of almost featureless snowscapes. With often so little color at hand, slight color shifts in some batches of film can produce disturbing effects, warranting the use of professional film with guaranteed stability.

All our equipment, including a good reserve of film and binoculars, plus a small assortment of basic survival gear (matches, signaling mirror, fishhooks, flashlight, penknife, sunscreen), fits in compact, custom-designed and homebuilt plywood cases (26 x 38 x 13 centimeters and 8.5 kilograms for Mark, and 26 x 32 x 12 centimeters and 7 kilograms for Tui). These are slightly more cumbersome than a fanny pack or knapsack, and not adequate for climbing, but are completely waterproof, dustproof, and virtually shockproof, without which our gear would simply not survive the rigorous maritime conditions to which it is routinely exposed. All items are fully accessible when the case is flipped horizontally on the hip, much as a cigarette or ice-cream vender on the street might do, without the need for a flat surface or even two free hands. When not in the case the camera is worn on a harness (made of shock cord and a couple of small fishing swivels) that crosses in the back and allows free movement from the chest to the eye but will not swing loosely. Nor will the camera drop should one of the jump-ring strap fastenings work loose.

Because of our unpremeditated, almost aimless approach, our attemps at using a tripod have always ended in frustration. The added encumbrance in the field, the delay in responding to a surprise situation, and the reduced flexibility in choosing the perfect angle have made us opt for shooting all our film hand-held, trying never to shoot below $\frac{1}{250}$ second with long lenses. Naturally, we sometimes pay the price in twilight situations when a time exposure is required, and we must contend with the even greater limitations of balancing the camera precariously on rock or ice.

Consideration for Other Species

In the photographer's paradise that is Antarctica, some visitors all too easily become carried away, forget the essence of the peaceful environment that brought them there, and behave despicably. Pressured perhaps by eagerness and time constraints, many photographers move brashly and threateningly, shattering the very harmony and beauty they are purporting to capture on film. Before moving forward one should invariably consider not only the subject of the intended shot, but also the nearness and reaction of other animals around. A low, crouching position to reduce your size difference with, say, penguins, and very slow, deliberate movements are usually all that is needed to win their trust. Once the photo session is over, the same care should be taken in departing; to a mother skua hunkered over her eggs, the lurching form of a departing human is just as alarming as an approaching one.

For some animals fear translates into flight, leaving eggs or chicks at the mercy of weather and predators. For others, such as the skua, the response is aggression. When aggression is aroused, it invariably means that we are at fault, and never should we retaliate by flailing or striking at the defensive parent, as this will only exacerbate the situation. Rather, we should depart as quickly and unobtrusively as possible. Photography does not, any more than science, give us the right to infringe upon the lives of the little beings we come so far to learn from and admire. In Antarctica all humans are visitors; it is the nonhumans whose personal space we are invading.

TUI DE ROY
MARK JONES

Maps

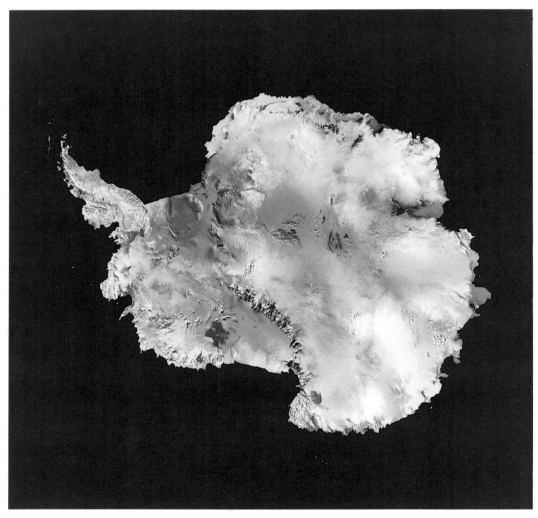

This computer-generated mosaic image of the Antarctic continent was prepared by the British National Remote Sensing Centre, using radiometric data gathered by NOAA polar-orbiting satellites between 1980 and 1983.

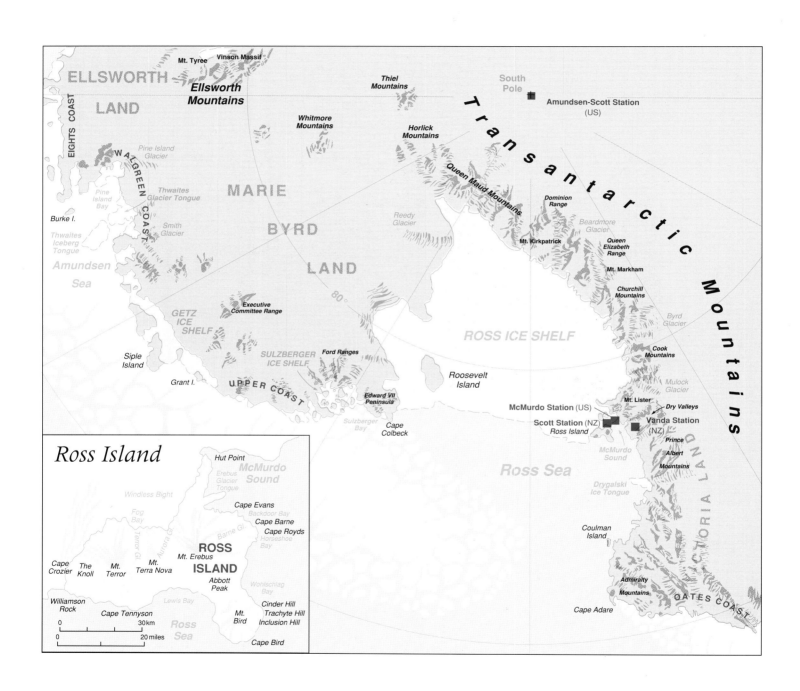

ELLSWORTH
LAND

EIGHTS COAST

Mt. Tyree Vinson Massif

**Ellsworth
Mountains**

Thiel
Mountains

South
Pole

Amundsen-Scott Station
(US)

Whitmore
Mountains

Horlick
Mountains

Queen Maud Mountains

W
A
L
G
R
E
E
N

C
O
A
S
T

Pine Island
Glacier

Pine
Island
Bay

Burke I.

Thwaites
Glacier Tongue

MARIE

Smith
Glacier

Thwaites
Iceberg
Tongue

BYRD

Reedy
Glacier

Amundsen
Sea

LAND

Dominion
Range

Beardmore
Glacier

Mt. Kirkpatrick

Queen
Elizabeth
Range

Mt. Markham

Churchill
Mountains

Byrd
Glacier

80°

Executive
Committee Range

GETZ
ICE
SHELF

ROSS ICE SHELF

Cook
Mountains

Siple
Island

SULZBERGER
ICE SHELF

Ford Ranges

Roosevelt
Island

Mulock
Glacier

Mt. Lister Dry Valleys

Grant I.

UPPER COAST

Edward VII
Peninsula

Sulzberger
Bay

Cape
Colbeck

McMurdo Station (US)

Scott Station (NZ)
Ross Island

Vanda Station
(NZ)

Prince
Albert
Mountains

McMurdo
Sound

Ross Sea

Drygalski
Ice Tongue

Coulman
Island

Admiralty
Mountains

OATES COAST

Cape Adare

T
r
a
n
s
a
n
t
a
r
c
t
i
c

M
o
u
n
t
a
i
n
s

VICTORIA LAND

Ross Island

Hut Point

McMurdo
Sound

Erebus
Glacier
Tongue

Windless Bight

Fog
Bay

Terror Gl.

Aurora Gl.

Barne Gl.

Cape Evans

Backdoor Bay

Cape Barne

Cape Royds

Horseshoe
Bay

Cape
Crozier

The
Knoll

Mt.
Terror

Mt.
Terra Nova

Mt. Erebus

**ROSS
ISLAND**

Abbott
Peak

Wohlschlag
Bay

Cinder Hill

Trachyte Hill

Inclusion Hill

Williamson
Rock

Cape Tennyson

Lewis Bay

Mt.
Bird

0   30km
0   20 miles

Ross
Sea

Cape Bird

219

Antarctic Peninsula

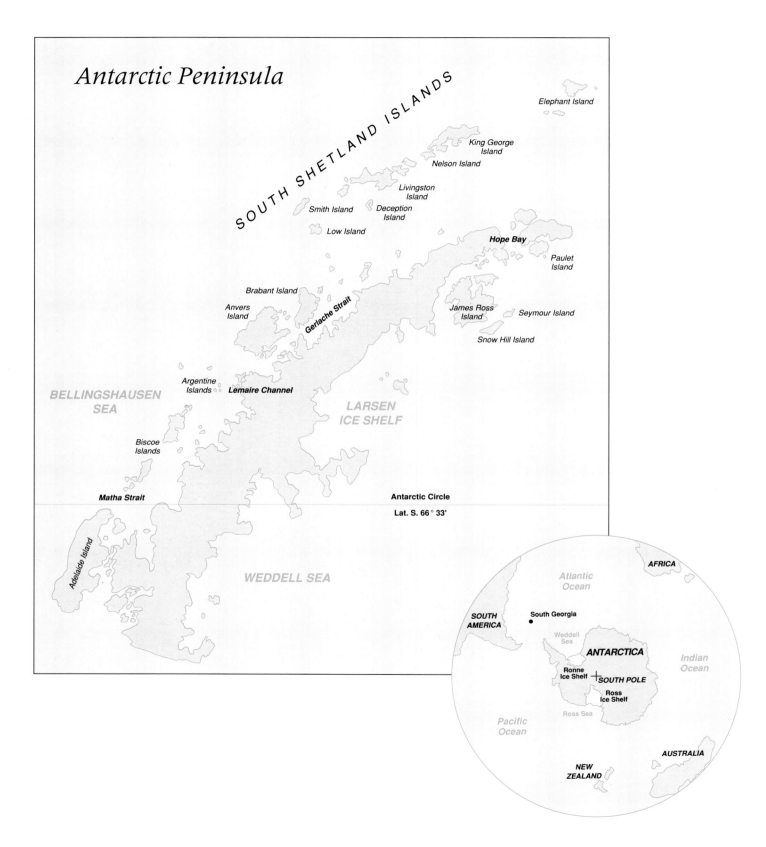

SOUTH SHETLAND ISLANDS

Elephant Island

King George Island

Nelson Island

Livingston Island

Smith Island

Deception Island

Low Island

Brabant Island

Anvers Island

Gerlache Strait

Hope Bay

Paulet Island

James Ross Island

Seymour Island

Snow Hill Island

Argentine Islands

Lemaire Channel

BELLINGSHAUSEN SEA

LARSEN ICE SHELF

Biscoe Islands

Matha Strait

Antarctic Circle

Lat. S. 66° 33'

Adelaide Island

WEDDELL SEA

AFRICA

Atlantic Ocean

SOUTH AMERICA

South Georgia

Weddell Sea

ANTARCTICA

Ronne Ice Shelf

SOUTH POLE

Indian Ocean

Ross Ice Shelf

Pacific Ocean

Ross Sea

AUSTRALIA

NEW ZEALAND

Notes on the Authors

RON NAVEEN is a naturalist, tour leader, writer, and photographer; the founder of Oceanites, a public foundation devoted to raising public consciousness about the world's living marine resources; and the editor of *The Antarctic Century* newsletter. His articles and photographs have appeared in the *Audubon Society Master Guide to Birding, Birding, American Birds, The Living Bird Quarterly,* and *National Geographic World.*

COLIN MONTEATH is a photographer, naturalist, mountain climber, expeditioneer, tour leader, and writer, based in New Zealand. He was the photographic editor and principal photographer for the internationally acclaimed *Reader's Digest Book of Antarctica.* His Alpine and Antarctic calendars have won a worldwide audience.

TUI DE ROY is a photographer, naturalist, tour leader, and writer, based in the Galapagos Islands. Her book *Galapagos: Islands Lost in Time* (Viking) has been a bestselling work for many years, and her photos and articles have appeared in many magazines, including *Smithsonian, National Wildlife, International Wildlife, Natural History, California Discovery,* and *Audubon.*

MARK JONES is a photographer, naturalist, tour leader, and writer, based in the Galapagos Islands. His photographs have appeared in *Smithsonian, National Wildlife, International Wildlife,* and *Natural History.*

Source Credits

Acknowledgment is gratefully made to the following sources for permission to include the quotations displayed throughout the text.

Excerpt from Apsley Cherry-Garrard's *The Worst Journey in the World* reprinted by permission of Chatto & Windus Ltd.

Excerpts from Annie Dillard's *Pilgrim at Tinker Creek* reprinted by permission of Harper & Row, Publishers, Inc. Copyright © 1974 by Annie Dillard.

Excerpts from Richard Byrd's *Alone* reprinted by permission of Island Press. Copyright © 1938 Richard E. Byrd, renewed 1966 by Marie A. Byrd.

Excerpt from *The Ice: A Journey to Antarctica* by Stephen Pyne reprinted by permission of the University of Iowa Press. Copyright © 1986 by University of Iowa Press.

Excerpts from Keith Shackleton's *Wildlife and Wilderness: An Artist's World* reprinted by permission of the author. Copyright © 1986 by Keith Shackleton.

Excerpt from Barry Lopez's *Arctic Dreams* reprinted by permission of Charles Scribner's Sons, an imprint of Macmillan Publishing Company. Copyright © 1986 by Barry Holstun Lopez.

Excerpt from George Gaylord Simpson's *Penguins Past and Present, Here and There* reprinted by permission of Yale University Press. Copyright © 1976 by Yale University.

Excerpt from Bernard Stonehouse's *Penguins* reprinted by permission of the author. Copyright © 1968 by Bernard Stonehouse.

Excerpt from Frank S. Todd's *The Sea World Book of Penguins* reprinted by permission of the author. Copyright © 1981 by Sea World, Inc.

Excerpts from Robert Cushman Murphy's *Oceanic Birds of South America* reprinted courtesy of the American Museum of Natural History.

(CM)

This book was produced by
the Smithsonian Institution Press

Separations and printing by
Amilcare Pizzi, S.p.A., Milan, Italy

Set in Meridien text with Caslon Open display type
by Graphic Composition Inc., Athens, Georgia

Edited by Duke Johns

Production coordinated by Kathleen Brown

Designed by Alan Carter

(TDR)

In Memoriam

On March 5, 1990, Giles Kershaw was killed in an aircraft accident in Antarctica. With his death a great beacon in Antarctic aviation was extinguished. During the course of fifteen Antarctic summers he flew over virtually the entire continent and pioneered the use of ice runways for wheeled aircraft. His work with the British Antarctic Survey in ski-equipped aircraft contributed greatly to the collection of scientific data. On one occasion, he planned and executed, against all odds, the rescue of scientists trapped on an ice floe. That rescue will long stand as a singular act of courage and dedication. Giles wanted Antarctica to be kept pristine so that it could continue to be a vital area of scientific study, and a place to be enjoyed by ecologically sensitive tourist expeditions. Those who come after him to this beautiful, unspoiled continent will owe him much.

D.C.W.